Jung Uncorked
Book Four

Marie-Louise von Franz, Honorary Patron

Studies in Jungian Psychology
by Jungian Analysts

Daryl Sharp, General Editor

JUNG UNCORKED

Rare Vintages from the Cellar
Of Analytical Psychology

BOOK FOUR

Decanted with commentaries by
DARYL SHARP

For all those in search of meaning, including myself, and especially my grandchildren: Dylan, Devon, Julian and Emily.
With special thanks to Rachel, MP, LKN and David Sharp.

Library and Archives Canada Cataloguing in Publication

Sharp, Daryl, 1936-
    Jung Uncorked: rare vintages from the cellar of
    analytical psychology / decanted with commentaries by Daryl Sharp.

(Studies in Jungian psychology by Jungian analysts; 126)

Includes bibliographical references and index.

ISBN 978-1-894574-21-1 (bk. 1).-- ISBN 978-1-894574-22-8 (bk. 2).--
ISBN 978-1-894574-24-2 (bk. 3).--ISBN 978-1-894574-27-3 (bk. 4).

1. Jungian psychology. I. Title. II. Series: Studies in Jungian
    Psychology by Jungian analysts; 120, 121, 123, 126

    BF173.J85S53 2008   150.19'54   C2007-905580-X

INNER CITY BOOKS
Box 1271, Station Q, Toronto, ON M4T 2P4, Canada.
Telephone (416) 927-0355 / Fax (416) 924-1814

Toll-free (Canada and U.S.): Tel. 1-888-927-0355 / Fax 1-888-924-1814

Web site: www.innercitybooks.net / E-mail: booksales@innercitybooks.net

Honorary Patron: Marie-Louise von Franz.
Publisher and General Editor: Daryl Sharp.
Senior Editor: Victoria B. Cowan.
Office Manager: Scott Milligen.

INNER CITY BOOKS was founded in 1980 to promote the
understanding and practical application of the work of C. G. Jung.

Printed and bound in Canada by Thistle Printing Company Ltd.

Contents

See final pages for descriptions of other Inner City titles

BOOK ONE *(published separately):*

BOOK TWO *(published separately):*

BOOK THREE (published separately):

The Symbolism of Wine

In so far as bread and wine are important products of culture, they do express a vital human striving. They represent a definite cultural achievement which is the fruit of attention, patience, industry, devotion, and laborious toil. The words "our daily bread" express man's anxious care for his existence. By producing bread he makes his life secure. But in so far as he "does not live by bread alone," bread is fittingly accompanied by wine, whose cultivation has always demanded a special degree of attention and much painstaking work. Wine, therefore, is equally an expression of cultural achievement. Where wheat and the vine are cultivated, civilized life prevails. But where agriculture and vine-growing do not exist, there is only the uncivilized life of nomads and hunters.

As to the special nature of these substances, bread is undoubtedly a food. There is a popular saying that wine "fortifies," though not in the same sense as food "sustains." It stimulates and "makes glad the heart of man'" by virtue of a certain volatile substance which has always been called "spirit." It is thus, unlike innocuous water, an "inspiriting" drink. . . . Bread therefore represents the physical means of subsistence, and wine the spiritual. [1]

---

[1] "Transformation Symbolism in the Mass," *Psychology and Religion: West and East,* CW 11, pars. 382, 384. (CW refers throughout to *The Collected Works of C. G. Jung)*

9

C. G. Jung gardening at his Bollingen tower (about 1957).

Preface

I have continued with this series for two reasons. First, I am besotted with the greatness of C. G. Jung. And second, I am in thrall to a psychological imperative to express myself in his company—present my thoughts on his various works in light of my own understanding and experience. This project is part and parcel of my own process.

This fourth instalment explicates one essay from each of volumes 9ii to 18 in Jung's *Collected Works,* with my commentaries on their psychological and contemporary significance. In the midst of a crazy-making extraverted world that defies all understanding, writing it has kept me close to a life-enhancing source of wisdom and sanity, and let me feel I'm doing something meaningful. I have also been heartened by the reception of the previous volumes of *Jung Uncorked,* which suggests that Jung's views on the structure and reality of the psyche are becoming more and more widely known and appreciated.

It bears repeating that I see myself as a conservative or "classical" Jungian analyst, that is, one who believes in the importance Jung gave to images from the unconscious and their influence on consciousness. I am an unabashed acolyte of Marie-Louise von Franz too.[2] In other words, I believe that Jung got it right. I leave it to others to go "beyond Jung" (if they feel they have the heft for it), as I continue to mine his

---

[2] See James A. Hall and Daryl Sharp, eds., *Marie-Louise von Franz: The Classic Jungian and the Classic JungianTradition.*

bedrock. I make no claim to be presenting here original research; rather I hew closely to the basic concepts of analytical psychology as Jung propounded them. Only the style and commentaries are uniquely my own, fostered by a love of Jung, fair ladies, music, fine wine, Eros and whimsy.

I am indebted to my editors, who save me from the excesses I can fall into when gripped by the "madness of the lead," as medieval alchemists described the fervor that assailed them in trying to understand what was happening in their retorts; i.e., how to apprehend the ineffable. That is how I feel when I tackle one of Jung's essays. But I soldier on, possibly for the greater good, but certainly for my own.

My intent is to inform and entertain, to reveal something of myself, and especially to stimulate readers to explore Jung's vintages on their own for further enlightenment.

The chapters here are purposely brief. Each one can be read in about twenty minutes, though its personal relevance may take a few days to sink in, and much longer to assimilate.

A few lines from the late Edward F. Edinger's tribute to his teacher, M. Esther Harding, express as well as anything the significance of Jung for our age:

> With the advent of Jung something truly new has appeared. Through his discovery of the reality of the psyche and of individuation as the process by which the individual realizes that reality, Jung has brought to birth a wholly new view of man and his world. This new view seems nothing less than the inauguration of a new aeon.[3]

Maktub, so it is written (Arabic).

---

[3] "M. Esther Harding, 1888-1971," *Spring 1972.*

9ii
The Shadow
(from *Aion,* CW 9ii, vintage 1948)

The shadow is a moral problem that challenges the whole ego-personality, for no one can become conscious of the shadow without considerable moral effort. To become conscious of it involves recognizing the dark aspects of the personality as present and real. This act is the essential condition for any kind of self-knowledge, and it therefore, as a rule, meets with considerable resistance. Indeed, self-knowledge as a psychotherapeutic measure frequently requires much painstaking work extending over a long period. [4]

You can say that again: "Self-knowledge requires much painstaking work extending over a long period"—indeed, more or less forever.

Alas, people seeking relief from psychic distress generally want and expect a quick fix. Hence the rise of such disciplines as "short-term psychotherapy," "mindfulness" and "behavior modification," all with a focus on alleviating symptoms. These are fine and good as far as they go in reducing suffering, but they leave untouched the underlying factors that plague the whole personality and which may unexpectedly erupt again, willy-nilly. Above all, they tend to ignore the pervasive influence of the unconscious in the overall psychic economy. Jung writes:

---

[4] "The Shadow," *Aion,* CW 9ii, par. 14.

The archetypes most clearly characterized from the empirical point of view are those which have the most frequent and the most disturbing influence on the ego. These are the *shadow,* the *anima,* and the *animus.*[5]

An earlier chapter in these books dealt at length with the latter two, the so-called contrasexual archetypes/complexes.[6] Here we will consider Jung's views on how the shadow is related, in a compensatory way, to the one-sided attitudes of ego-consciousness.

Emotional discomfort is a hallmark of the shadow. Whenever something we have done, are doing, or think of doing causes us to feel guilty, ashamed, embarrassed or dumb, we can be sure the shadow side of the personality is involved. The shadow is by definition the polar opposite of the bright, intelligent, honorable and morally responsible persona with which the ego tends to identify.

I must back up a little here, to remind the reader that the persona is a complex primarily conditioned by culture and environment. It is the aspect of ourselves that we generally show to others—charming, enlightened, tolerant and socially acceptable. It is both a mask and a defense, at times helpful and necessary, but not who we really are.

The persona aims to live up to what is expected, what is "proper." It is a useful bridge socially and an indispensable protective covering; without a persona, we are simply too vulnerable to the outside world. We regularly cover up our inferiorities with a persona, since we do not like our weaknesses to be seen. Civilized society depends on interactions between

---

[5] Ibid., par. 13.

[6] See "The Syzygy: Anima and Animus," *Jung Uncorked,* Book Two, pp. 10ff.

people through the persona. But it is psychologically unhealthy to identify with it, to believe we are "nothing but" the person we show to others.

Generally speaking, the shadow is less civilized, more primitive, cares little for social propriety. What is of value to the persona is anathema to the shadow, and vice versa. Hence the shadow and the persona function in a compensatory way: the brighter the light, the darker the shadow. The more one identifies with the persona—which in effect is to deny that one has a shadow—the more trouble one will have with the unacknowledged other side of the personality, which may unexpectedly put us to shame.

Thus the shadow constantly challenges the morality of the persona, and, to the extent that ego-consciousness identifies with the persona, the shadow also threatens the ego. In the process of psychological development that Jung called individuation, disidentification from the persona and the conscious assimilation of the shadow go hand in hand. The ideal is to have an ego strong enough to acknowledge both the persona and the shadow without identifying with either.

In this day and age, the notion of a persona is pretty well understood, though it may soon be overtaken by the term "avatar," traditionally a spiritual guide but now common in the so-called metaverse (metaphorical, virtual universes like Second Life and Facebook) or dating sites on the Internet. Indeed, one's avatar in this sense may simply personify one's shadow, or at least as much of it as one is comfortable revealing to strangers.

Psychologically speaking, the shadow is everywhere—behind the scenes like the phantom of the opera, the fly in the ointment, the skeleton in the closet. There is nothing too nefarious for the shadow to have a hand in—tax evasion, extramarital affairs, fraud, arson, spousal and child abuse, rape, murder, religious and political strife, and on and on. In short, *the shadow is everywhere.* That is the inescapable reality behind Jung's oft-quoted admonition:

> We need more psychology. We need more understanding of human nature, because the only real danger that exists is man himself. He is the great danger, and we are pitifully unaware of it. We know nothing of man, far too little. His psyche should be studied, because we are the origin of all coming evil.[7]

There is no way to escape the insidious influence of the shadow except to become conscious of it. To be aware of what we are capable of does not make us invulnerable, but it can prepare us for the unexpected scenarios of life. A harmless flirtation can escalate; a few juggled figures can land us in jail. That is the shadow at work.

But hold your horses. The shadow is not all bad news. Besides unacceptable impulses, repressed or suppressed, the shadow may also contain ignored or forgotten potential. I mean to say, the shadow can be a destructive influence, but it may also be creative. That is one essential difference between Jung's view of the unconscious and that of Freud, who saw the unconscious (or "id") as entirely negative, a repository of repressed childhood sexual desires.

I think of Jocelyn, an attractive thirty-year-old, underpaid

---

[7] "The 'Face to Face' Interview," 1959, in William McGuire and R. F. C. Hull, eds. *C. G. Jung Speaking: Interviews and Encounters*, p. 436.

and overworked as a "gofer" in the film industry. She had barely finished high school and felt trapped in her situation without more education. She came to me with the following dream:

> Where am I? On a cloud?! Yes, I am floating high above the earth with the wings of an angel. An elegant gentleman approaches and hands me a cap and gown. "You forgot these," he says.

Well I can tell you I was nearly overcome with delight. Jocelyn was wary; she had not yet come to trust the imagery of her dreams. I saw the "elegant gentleman" as a helpful animus figure, and encouraged her to think of going back to school. A few months later she enrolled in a pre-university make-up course, and within a year she was accepted into a Bachelor of Arts program in literature. She thanked me. I bowed to her unconscious.

The shadow has a mercurial quality—it assumes different shapes in its hosts. In a chemistry lab, touch a blob of the silvery element mercury and it breaks into pieces that scurry off in all directions. That is what the shadow does, putting us at odds with ourselves.

*

I seldom think about the past, and I do not worry myself about the future. What is left? Well, I am focused on expressing what occupies my mind in the present—what is right in front of me. There are a multitude of issues I could bring to the fore, ego-concerns, but I hesitate to mention the obvious and the trivial, which both alike bore me stupid.

So saying, I want to bring my mother into this narrative.

This may sound odd or inappropriate, even goofy, but I will tell you how it came about.

Some weeks ago I plucked *War and Peace* off the library shelf, having convinced myself that it was time to read Tolstoy. Well, I stuck with it for 150 pages (out of 700) and finally gave up. What a turgid mess of potage: aristocratic buffoonery, military arrogance, coquettish ladies with wide-open bodices but lower regions veiled by stylish beaded reticules (whatever they were) and minds occupied by gossip and the latest fad at court. I mean I had to wonder why this book has been deemed a "classic," though I concede that I was simply not prepared for its sweep and grandeur. (I have since seen the opera, which I enjoyed.)

I turned instead to Carol Shields' *The Stone Diaries,* which I had started some time ago but laid aside, not then ready for the candid, open-hearted recounting of a woman's life in many different voices, including, of course, her shadowy thoughts, which now quite bowled me over. I became completely engaged with this Pulitzer Prize winner. In the midst of this enchantment I dreamed of my mother, who died some twenty years ago and who has not since weighed heavily in my thoughts until I became seriously engrossed in this essay and writing this chapter.

I recall my mother, née Marion Weist, as a stereotypical woman of the 1930s, 40s and 50s. Her peasant grandparents had immigrated to Canada in the 1880s from a German-speaking enclave in Odessa. It was then known as "White Russia". My Gramma Weist never learned to read or write English, but her husband, Martin by name, became proficient enough to land a job as a typesetter on the *Regina Leader Post* newspaper. They anchored a happy extended family in Regina, prairie capital of Saskatchewan in western Canada. Among my fondest memories are Sunday dinners with them all, followed by polka dancing or bingo, canasta, euchre or poker. My gramma knew her numbers very well and made sure I did too. Or else we took turns on the Ouija board or reading tea leaves, which is a whole other story from my shadowy past, best saved for the novel I'll never write. My gramma's folklore wisdom began and ended with the mantra, "Never put anything in your ear but your elbow." She was fat, loving and always happy, except for the time her twenty-five-year-old daughter Eva (my mom's younger sister) died from a botched tonsillectomy. Gramma took to her bed and cried for four whole days. I have never since heard of such keening except among primitive tribes. I was seven at the time and didn't know what was happening, but I was lost in the family grief.

My mother was the kind of woman portrayed in television sitcoms of the period—selfless, modest, unassuming, guileless, completely devoted to husband and two smart-ass sons who teased her unmercifully. She clipped recipes from the *Reader's Digest* and *Ladies Home Companion,* and gave me what for if I didn't finish my breakfast porridge or came home late from school. She had been a chorus-line dancer before wedding my father in 1932, but that oomph was gone by the time I became sentient. Except, however, I do recall one night when my father, then a corporal in the Royal Canadian Air Force, came home plastered, and in a snit she tore all the buttons off his uniform. I remember too that she sewed them all back on in the morning before he left. And polished his boots.

That's the kind of wife she was, and very pretty too—not Garbo or Dietrich seductive, more like the laid-back, mild-mannered Lillian Gish. In my waiting room there hangs a picture of my mom with two-year-old me on her lap. I adored my mother, and as a kid I used to creep up behind her and untie her apron strings, just to see her laugh with joy. I wore her chorus girl outfit on Halloween until I was twelve. "Leave the dishes in the sink, Ma" was a song written to give her a break from unrelenting domestic chores, about which she never complained. In those Great Depression years, money was always tight, and I was five years old before she took me to the local soda fountain for a special treat—my first taste of ice cream. A Freudian might have a field day with all that—wrap it in a neat Oedipal bow, but I accept it as a just-so story.

Okay, so I have a mother complex. And who has not? Only now, in my senior years, do I wonder what her inner life was like. Oh, I do feel badly about my neglect of her! My heart aches and I am ashamed to realize how I took her affectionate concern for granted and never wondered who was there behind it. You see, her life was lived on a persona level, always for others. Whatever personal potential she had—let's call it her shadow in this context—never came to light, and I never gave her unlived life a thought. Shame on me.

I am familiar enough with the masculine shadow, but I can hardly fathom the other side of women, which to this day bemuses me. Of course, this does not prevent me from loving them to pieces. Come to think of it, when I was growing up, not a day would pass when I didn't hear my father tell my mother he loved her, at which she beamed. They were a model of a happy, solid relationship.

As I have said elsewhere, I like living alone, but a loving woman trumps solitude. However, more to the point here, it is the mysterious, shadowy spark that ignites a woman's desire for intimacy with a particular man that puzzles and eludes me. I am not even sure if that spark is properly described as "shadowy"; it may be an expression of their essence, for all I know. But I can hardly count the number of women in my practice who have confided their physical indifference to their mates and lust for someone else.

My ignorance of the female shadow is only mitigated these days by the tender confidences of my paramour (MP) and those women brave enough to reveal themselves in art, song or books. Off the top of my head I think of Virginia Woolf, Billie Holiday, Janis Joplin, Grace Slick, Stevie Nicks, Sylvia Plath, Alice Munroe, Carol Shields of course, Barbra Streisand, Tina Turner, Madonna, and don't forget Emily Dickenson. Go ahead; compile your own list of shadow-conscious women. I dare say there are and have been thousands, mostly unsung outside their immediate family or circle of friends.

In practice, as noted elsewhere in this series, the shadow and everything associated with it is virtually synonymous with unlived life. "There must be more to life than this," is a remark heard often enough in the consulting room. And it is true. All that I consciously am and aspire to be effectively shuts out what I might be, could be, *also am*. Some of what I "also am" has been repressed because it was or is unacceptable to oneself or others, and some is simply unrealized potential—none of it easy to differentiate.

Of course, in my analytic practice I come across people with absent or negative mothers. Unless I can establish a degree of rapport with such clients, who are often tied up inside with resentment, bitterness, abandonment and a pervasive desire for revenge, I am useless to them, for my approach to life's dilemmas is not as a soothsayer or spiritual director or hit man. I am someone who accompanies those individuals on the path they intuit for themselves. Though I may on occasion give a prod or two, I cannot save people from themselves. This is as much as I can say about my "technique," which in fact is simply an attitude that takes the unconscious seriously. And this may go on for months or even years, until the client says something like, "Thanks Doc, it's been real and unreal; I think I can manage now on my own."

Through introspection, we can become aware of shadow aspects of our own personality, but we may still resist them or fear their influence. And even where they are known and would be welcome, they are not readily available to the conscious will. For instance, my intuition may be shadowy—primitive and unadapted—so I cannot call it up when it's needed. I may know that feeling is required in a particular situation but for the life of me can't muster it. I want to enjoy the party but my carefree extraverted side has vanished. I may know I'm due for some introversion, but the lure of the bright lights is just too strong.

The shadow does not necessarily demand equal time with the ego, but for a balanced personality it does require recognition. For the introvert this may involve an occasional night on the town—against his "better judgment." For the extravert it might involve—in spite of herself—an evening staring at the wall.

In general, the person whose shadow is repressed gives the

impression of being dull and stodgy. This is particularly evident in a man's attitude toward women. The loyal, persona-
identified man ignores or suppresses his instinctive reactions
to females other than his partner. The shadow-conscious man
accepts and enjoys the reality that his psyche is host to a
harem of lovely ladies, while being wary of acting on his er-
rant erotic impulses. On the whole, I think a man's women
friends appreciate this as a measure of his character—though
it may be something one recognizes but does not say out loud.
On the other hand, nowadays it has been called "emotional
infidelity" when a man or woman has a close friend other than
their mates. Nonsense, I say! Call them loverNots and enjoy.
Of course, one's partner may have his or her own insecurities,
but that is another story.

Needless to say, this is a man-centric view of male-female
relationships. Women can write their own books if they have
the heart for it.

I don't know what it's like with a woman, but for a man the
feeling of being in love after making love is so generally
known that it hardly bears mentioning. Not so widely known
is that this feeling is often tinged with more than a touch of
gratitude for having been received back into the source, as it
were, safely enveloped by the warm embrace of the Great
Mother. More than one besotted man has married the apparent
hostess of such "oceanic" feelings—and not always to his or
her regret, divorce rates notwithstanding.

The vagina, with its fascinating folds and ravines, is an in-
exhaustibly rich mystery to a man. It is also a woman's not-

so-secret weapon in the battle of the sexes.[8] Pudendum trumps phallus any day, perhaps because of that oceanic feeling it elicits when penetrated, and vice versa, for all I know. It is not, however, an impersonal body organ; it has character and integrity. That is why rape is such a traumatic violation of self. Straight-talking analyst Albert Kreinheder describes the vulva as "a cushioned, silky, fleecy place, springy like a tiger's paw, slippery and gorged with blood, inviting my entry."[9] Well, that is about as far as you can get from the legendary fantasy of the fearsome *vagina dentata* (toothed vagina).[10]

It is widely believed that it is essentially hormonic harmony that fuels romantic fantasies, and that may be so. Love at first sight happens often and I have heard of love at first hug too. But it is not common knowledge that emotional reactions toward others are rooted in one's personal psychology and may have little to do with the other person. This is due to the phenomenon of projection, whereby we see in others unconscious aspects of ourselves—traits or qualities we are aware of only dimly, if at all. Listen to what men say or sing about women: "You've captured my soul," "Can't live without you," "My one-and-only love," and so on—and pity the poor woman who is prey to these sentiments and falls for them without a grain of salt. Now don't get me wrong. I am entirely in favor of projection in the service of life and love.

---

[8] The classical model for modern bedroom farce is Aristophanes' play, *Lysistrata* (411 B.C.), in which the eponymous heroine enlists the agreement of her Greek sisters to withhold sex from their men until they end the Peloponnesian War.

[9] *Body and Soul,* p. 45.

[10] The Austrian psychoanalyst Otto Rank first identified this image in 1924, in his book *The Trauma of Birth,* as a widespread cause of anxiety among neurotic men.

Projection is a fact of life. We do not consciously make projections; we meet with them. In Jung's pithy sentence, "Projections change the world into the replica of one's own unknown face."[11] We are powerless when in the grip of a projection, good or bad, and we rarely comprehend what hit us. Alas, as Jung was wont to emphasize, the unconscious *is* unconscious. All the same, in the Jungian world we are not foolish enough to speak of projection unless there are obvious problems in a relationship. We do not stir a pot that isn't boiling over, and who among us is fit to discern "true love" from projection? It's a mug's game. But as I said, I am one hundred percent in favor of projection and romance. Indeed, they will be my downfall, if not already.

But what, you may ask, does romance have to do with the shadow anyway? Well, that is a fair question.

I think that all a fella really needs to be happy is "a kiss to build a dream on." In other words, a little show of Eros is all it takes to get the fantasy mill churning. This is his fundamental reality, though he may fudge it with scholarly or jockular talk. A woman's reality is unknown to me, but possibly similar, except for the jock talk, though I'm not even sure of that.

I mean, you gotta be pretty cynical to think love is just an illusion. It is that, of course, but hardly the whole story.

Jung noted that the opposite of love is not hate, but power.[12] I agree but that still leaves a lot of nuances to be accounted for: power for what purpose, love of what and who and why? Such reflections can easily lead to a miasma of doubt and

---

[11] "The Shadow," *Aion,* CW 9ii, par. 17.
[12] *Two Essays,* CW 7, par. 78.

conflict, which as a matter of fact is good for the soul but not often a happy time for the ego.

Come to think of it, maybe cynicism is the flip side of love; which is to say that someone who is cynical, world-weary, is ripe for falling in love. It is hard to find any man, or woman, at any age, who fell in love with a blank slate. There is always a hook (something in the other that elicits a certain passion), and an ineluctable draw toward fulfilling one's personal destiny, articulated or not.

I think of my client Roger, so delighted one night by his wife's enthusiastic response that he said, "You aren't always like this; what's up?" She threw him out of bed and he charged her with assault. They later divorced, to no one's surprise but his.

Well, there's only one way out of this cul de sac—a little song and dance. How about this:

> You made me love you
> I didn't want to do it, I didn't want to do it
> You made me love you and all the time you knew it
> I guess you always knew it.
> You made me happy sometimes, you made me glad
> But there were times, dear, you made me feel so bad
> You made me sigh for, I didn't want to tell you
> I didn't want to tell you
> I want some love that's true, yes I do, deed I do, you know I do
> Give me, give me, give me what I cry for
> You know you got the brand of kisses that I'd die for
> You know you made me love you.[13]

---

[13] "You Made Me Love You," made popular by Al Jolson, Judy Garland, Doris Day, Patsy Cline and others; music by James V. Monaco, lyrics by Joseph

Many months ago, gripped by midnight madness, I offered to give a seminar for the local Jungian community called "The Love Syndrome." It was duly scheduled for a year ahead and registrations poured in, but after sober thought I canceled the event. It just seemed too pretentious, and I quailed at the prospect of having to contain so many complexes.

Now, there are those who eschew romance on account of potential suffering. I am aware of their concerns—having been there myself—but I am not one of them. Knock me down and I get up, and fall right over again. Sinatra swings it gently like this:

Moon River, wider than a mile
I'm crossing you in style someday
You dream maker, you heartbreaker
Wherever you're going I'm going your way

Two drifters off to see the world
There's such a lot of world to see
We're after the same rainbows end
Waiting round the bend
My huckleberry friend, Moon River
And me.[14]

The simple truth is that I would rather be in love than be in charge. And my shadow agrees with that.

It is well known that Jung was both appreciative and critical of the Christian ethic.[15] In terms of the shadow, this is nowhere more evident than in the following letter he wrote to a

---

McCarthy; ASCAP.

[14] "Moon River," from *Frank Sinatra: Romance,* music and lyrics by Henry Mancini and Johnny Mercer; BMI.

[15] See John P. Dourley, *The Illness That We Are: A Jungian Critique of Christianity,* esp. chap. 1, "Jung's Ambivalence Toward Christianity," pp. 7ff.

young Christian woman, referring to the words of Jesus in Mathew 25:

> I admire Christians,
> Because when you see someone who is hungry or thirsty,
> You see Jesus.
> When you welcome a stranger, someone who is "strange,"
> You welcome Jesus.
> When you clothe someone who is naked, you clothe Jesus.
> What I do not understand, however,
> Is that Christians never seem to recognize Jesus
> In their own poverty.
> You always want to do good to the poor outside you
> And at the same time you deny the poor person
> Living inside you.
> Why can't you see Jesus in your own poverty,
> In your own hunger and thirst?
> In all that is "strange" inside you:
> In the violence and the anguish that are beyond your control!
> You are called to welcome all this, not *to deny* its existence,
> But to accept that it is there and to meet Jesus there.[16]

Well, no wonder Jung wrote an extensive piece on "Christ, a Symbol of the Self,"[17] which I commend to all those seeking a bridge between their atheistic beliefs and Christianity.

---

[16] See Jean Vanier, *Befriending the Stranger,* pp. 59f. (original source unavailable).

[17] See *Aion,* CW 9ii, pars. 68ff.

10
The Undiscovered Self

(from *Civilization in Transition,* CW 10, vintage 1957)

Just as man, as a social being, cannot in the long run exist without a tie to the community, so the individual will never find the real justification for his existence and his own spiritual and moral autonomy anywhere except in an extramundane principle capable of relativizing the overpowering influence of external factors. The individual who is not anchored in God can offer no resistance on his own resources to the physical and moral blandishments of the world. For this he needs the evidence of inner, transcendent experience which alone can protect him from the otherwise inevitable submersion in the mass.[18]

I am often overwhelmed by my self-imposed tasks. Take this book, for instance. No one is waiting for my take on this essay or any others in Jung's CW. But I continue to grapple with them, ponder and lose sleep, feel inadequate. However, as they say, it goes with the territory.

This particular essay was actually my first acquaintance with Jung. It was 1960. I was a very young man, a self-important "struggling writer" in London, England, when I came across it, a slim paperback edition, in a used bookstore. I bought it on impulse for one shilling. Now, some fifty years later, I am at pains to recall its initial impact, which as a mat-

---

[18] "The Undiscovered Self," *Civilization in Transition,* CW 10, par. 511.

ter of fact did not bear any noticeable fruit in my life until a few years later. But perhaps that is precisely why I have chosen this essay from the many others in CW 10—to conjure up the excitement and enthusiasm I felt when I first read it.

Psychologically naïve, I could not for ages fathom the difference between lower-case self and capital Self. But the very title implied that I didn't know myself, however spelled, and perhaps that is what hooked me—my own ignorance.

In those long-ago days, I was still attached to the collective by an umbilical cord about two thousand miles long. I had left Procter & Gamble (and a 1956 Ford Thunderbird convertible) for a fantasy life in Europe, and I was going nowhere but down. In time I fell helplessly in love, convinced her to marry and we had a child, then another and another. I think I was a decent father, but being a "momma's boy" I was a quintessential *puer* and not much of a husband.[19] I know this only in retrospect, for I was extraverted at the time and not much given to introspection.

So, I had left the corporate world behind, spurred on by such mid-century anti-establishment classics as William Whyte's *The Organization Man* and Philip Wylie's wildly acerbic *Generation of Vipers* with its passionate polemic against "Momism." However, I suffered greatly from the loss of community and a value system I had grown up with and heartily embraced for a couple of years as an up-and-coming, bushy-tailed young executive—values based on materialism,

---

[19] For the definitive study of this syndrome, see Marie-Louise von Franz, *The Problem of the Puer Aeternus.* Presumedly, the puer/senex dyad is latent throughout life, and the energies of one or other manifest when appropriate to balance our ego-conscious imbalance. See also Ann Yeoman, *Now or Neverland: Peter Pan and the Myth of Eternal Youth.*

ambition, success, etc.; everything we loosely call, even in Canada, "the American way of life." I had rebelled *against,* but I wasn't *for* anything but myself—individualism of the most egregious kind.[20] I was not interested in politics or religion, or any other "ism," and without a new foundation to replace the old order, I hovered in mid-air, rootless. I was as ripe for cult-conversion as any country hick just off the bus in New York. God knows how I escaped that, or even if I did.

I wrote and wrote, but the world did not welcome my turgid tomes, and rightly so, for I had little inside me worth writing about. I acted like a clever fellow, and even believed I was as I pecked away on my portable Smith-Corona in a hut at the foot of the garden, but I felt like the Beatles' nowhere man, making all his nowhere plans for nobody—"doesn't have a point of view, knows not where he's going to. . . ."

I had left my well-paid junior-executive job at P & G simply because I found it "meaningless"—though I was fuzzy as to what that meant (except for the banality of the products I was obliged to promote), and for a long time I found nothing to replace it. I was floating, bereft.

In Europe, falling among literary friends, I was soon seduced by, and found temporary solace in, such iconic writers as Kafka, Kierkegaard, Nietzsche, Rilke, Dostoyevsky, Camus, Henry Miller, Samuel Beckett and a dozen others of that ilk. Their work excited me no end, but the best I could do was mimic them. They buoyed me for a time; I could read a line

---

[20] Curiously, the words "individualism" and "individuation" do not appear in this essay. The difference, to be very brief, is that the former bespeaks a "me first" outsider attitude, while individuation is a process of becoming who you were meant to be, within and related to a collective. (See below, pp. 100ff., and my *Jung Lexicon: A Primer of Terms & Concepts* for fuller descriptions.)

and write for two pages, but their outlook on life was essentially negative and ultimately too bleak (except of course for Henry Miller's bawdy novels) to sustain the fun-loving WASP I was, flirtatiously haunting Chelsea pubs, hitchhiking around Europe, or making out with English lovelies during coffee-breaks on the roof deck of Harrod's department store, where I worked for a time packing books. It was the age of so-called free love, after all, though in the long run I and some others of my generation paid a pretty psychic penny for our cavalier attitude toward Eros. Not that I regret an ounce of those premarital sown oats, not on your nelly. That would be forsaking my essentially middle-class roots and my first-grown-up lover, a spirited colleen from Winnipeg who liked dancing and me loving her from behind. I was truly reluctant to leave her, and cried as I sailed off on a freighter to my problematic future in Europe.

Into this void of a personality dropped C. G. Jung and "The Undiscovered Self" for the princely sum of one shilling (about U.S. 25 cents then), which incidentally was the average hourly wage of an English manual laborer in the early 1960s. I know this bit of trivia because I dug ditches between stints of teaching in those horrid British secondary-modern schools, where half the kids were hooligans and the other half asleep. (Another chapter in my never-to-be novel.)[21]

Well, I finally became bored eating my heart out in that hut, and in the mid-sixties talked my way into a graduate program at the newly-founded University of Sussex in Brighton. It involved literature and philosophy under the umbrella title

---

[21] Frank McCourt has chronicled better than I could this frustrating experience, albeit in the New York school system, in his novels *'Tis* and *Teacher Man.*

of "The Modern European Mind," just my meat. This resulted in an M.A. thesis entitled "In Search of the Self," an immodestly ambitious comparative study of the work of D.H. Lawrence, Kierkegaard and Jung. It might as well have been called "In Search of Meaning," for that was what I was really after. And in Jung's thought-provoking essay I found it, in spades. Without a bye your leave, and hardly noticing it, from an existentialist I became an essentialist.[22]

The passage that heads this chapter is the one that struck me most forcefully on initial reading. *Extramundane principle! Transcendent experience!* Wow. These were new concepts to me. I had written about "echoing depths," but I was talking through my hat—I didn't really have a clue what I meant by that. Now I realized that the writers I admired were involved in mining their own unconscious. And indeed, it was a sense of the transcendent (a new word to me) that was notably absent from my irreligious upbringing (except for storytelling at United Church Sunday School and bingo in church basements with my gramma). Transcendent!—something of, but at the same time outside of, myself to believe in and to experience, something beyond the daily grind, something other-worldly, even irrational. I might have found this in other ways or other writers if I had known what to look for, but I didn't, and only serendipitously chanced upon it in Jung's celebration of the individual, real man as opposed to the corporate, statistical man I had been conditioned by my culture to become.

---

[22] I am indebted to analyst J. Gary Sparks for this concise distinction: "The existentialist says we create ourselves. The essentialist says we discover ourselves." *(At the Heart of Matter: Synchronicity and Jung's Spiritual Testament,* pp. 125f.)

I have since realized how difficult it is for anyone to escape the influence of the environment they grow up in. I think "brain-washing" is not too strong a term for what we are inculcated to expect and want as adults. It is an unconscious endeavor in tune with the culture

In my early working life, being the editor of P & G's in-house magazine *Moonbeams* was fun and interesting and moreover conferred a persona-status I found hard to do without. I was twenty-one years old. My only previous work experience was a summer job as a short-order cook at the local café. Then suddenly, straight out of university, I was recruited by P & G to be Director of Public Relations for Canada. They flew me to head office in Cincinnati and gave me a Leica camera. I was captain of the company bowling team. I had stock options, benefits and a pension plan, a secure future. I had a midnight blue suit and a key to the executive washroom! I was starting at the top. Now I ask you, talk about inflation. For some months, I was cock of the walk.

When I forsook that job, my father, who had worked his way up through the ranks of the Canadian Air Force to become an officer, said sadly, "Son, you'll always regret it." And for some months I did. Between excitements at the opera, ballet and in pubs, I was homesick and thought of going back to resume my "proper place" in my culture, my society. It was my first *crise de foie* (crisis of faith).

"Struggling writer" just didn't cut it—harder work and few outer rewards. I didn't know then that as a Capricorn I was fated by the stars (or say the gods, why not) to reap a harvest later in life.[23] However, I continued to practice my craft and eventually persuaded London publishers to pay me for editing manuscripts and compiling indexes, a tedious and exacting task I had never done before.

In this essay, writing at the height of the Cold War, Jung offers no easy solutions to the contemporary crisis in world affairs. Instead he declares that the alternative to world annihilation depends not upon mass movements for good or on idealistic appeals to reason, but rather upon a recognition of the existence of good and evil in every individual and a true understanding of the secular soul. "The Undiscovered Self" is, as the *New York Times Book Review* noted at the time, "a passionate plea for individual integrity."[24]

Well, I was a complete novice in the field of psychology. My studies in mathematics and physics had left little room for the humanities. I knew nothing of Freud's ubiquitous influence in the modern world. Shoot! I had hardly even heard of the sub- or unconscious except as a garbage bin of repressed wishes to sleep with one parent or the other. I was not an intellectual, that's for sure, but I prided myself on being a scientist and a reasonable "child of the Enlightenment." Logos prevailed in my world; sex too, but how was a young fella to learn of Eros?

Imagine, even at the time I abandoned physics for journalism, Ernest Hemingway's laconic style, more or less bereft of adjectives, was the model for good writing, called objectivity: who, what, why, where and when, but little feeling except,

---

[23] As it happens, my astrological birth-mates include Richard Nixon and Marie-Louise von Franz. It's what you call a mixed blessing.

[24] Back cover, Mentor edition, 1958.

maybe, if you were prescient, between the lines. North America in the mid-twentieth century was a macho, patriarchal world where the feminine in general was of little account outside the kitchen and the bedroom—but only on the surface, while underneath, behind the curtains, women held the reins of power as they always have since time immemorial on account of that magically inspiriting yoni. Women may roll their eyes, but that's the way I see it. Most men are just large children, easy prey to their instincts and need for mothering.

Anyway, all in all, Jung's essay was for me a wake-up call, an epiphany of sorts, for its essential message was that the visible, everyday world is not all there is, and that the hidden side of ourselves, the unconscious, of which we know very little, has a greater say in our attitudes and behavior patterns than most of us realize. It is true that Freud was there first, though not *the* first,[25] and not for me.

I think "The Undiscovered Self" speaks especially to those who have lost, or never had, a religious or creedal belief. Jung acknowledges that organized religion, of whatever stripe, has traditionally been a counterbalance to mass-mindedness as well as the middleman, so to speak, between a Higher Power and our mundane concerns. Nor does he dispute the fact that Church dogma, whatever atrocities it may have been responsible for over the ages, has been the saving factor in many an individual life. But he distinguishes a creed from a religion:

A creed gives expression to a definite collective belief, whereas the word *religion* [from Latin *religere,* meaning the careful observation and consideration of irrational factors] ex-

---

[25] See Henri F. Ellenberger, *The Discovery of the Unconscious.*

presses a subjective relationship to certain metaphysical, extramundane factors. A creed is a confession of faith intended chiefly for the world at large and is thus an intramundane affair, while the meaning and purpose of religion lie in the relationship of the individual to God (Christianity, Judaism, Islam) or to the path of salvation and liberation (Buddhism). From this basic fact all ethics is derived, which without the individual's responsibility before God can be called nothing more than conventional morality.

. . . A creed coincides with the established Church or, at any rate, forms a public institution whose members include not only true believers but vast numbers of people who can only be described as "indifferent" in matters of religion and who belong to it simply by force of habit. Here the difference between a creed and a religion becomes palpable. [26]

Indeed, elsewhere Jung describes religion in terms of a certain attitude of mind—"the attitude peculiar to a consciousness which has been changed by experience of the numinosum"—the awesome or holy unknown.[27] By all accounts, such personal experience is rather rare since the Middle Ages, and consequently the equivalent of religious authority is relegated by default to the State. Jung writes:

The policy of the State is exalted to a creed, the leader or party boss becomes a demigod beyond good and evil, and his votaries are honoured as heroes, martyrs, apostles, missionaries. There is only *one* truth and beside it no other. It is sacrosanct and above criticism. Anyone who thinks differently is a heretic, who, as we know from history, is threatened with all manner of unpleasant things.[28]

---

[26] "The Undiscovered Self," *Civilization in Transition,* CW 10, pars. 507f.

[27] "Psychology and Religion," *Psychology and Religion,* CW 11, par. 9.

[28] "The Undiscovered Self," *Civilization in Transition,* CW 10, par. 511.

That passage obviously refers to dictatorships, but it is arguably applicable in democracies too. The recent U.S. presidential Bush years come to mind, as does President Dwight D. Eisenhower's warning in the 1950s about the military-industrial "complex," though Ike might not have realized that his words had psychological overtones.

Well, there are many other cogent passages I could quote here, for it is a long essay, about fifty pages; but I think I have given you the gist of its overall import, which is that when the collective rules, individuality will inevitably be driven to the wall. I have little more to say about it, except that it prepared me, well in advance, to accept my improbable evolution into a Jungian analyst and publisher of books by other analysts. A life with meaning was Jung's unwitting gift to me, and "The Undiscovered Self" was my first intimation of it.

And by the way, in a subtle twist of the pickled finger of fate, the house I now live and work in is just around the corner from the office I had at P & G. Synchronicity, anyone?

Well, that was almost sixty years ago. I think that if I had stayed with P & G I would either be head of the company now or dead. Either way I'd be in hell, where I may be anyway, but at least on my own terms.

11
Yoga and the West

(from *Psychology and Religion: West and East,*
CW 11, vintage 1936)

I say to whomsoever I can: "Study yoga—you will learn an infinite amount from it—but do not try to apply it, for we Europeans are not so constituted that we apply these methods correctly, just like that. An Indian guru can explain everything and you can imitate everything. But do you know *who* is applying the yoga? In other words, do you know who you are and how you are constituted?"[29]

In so far as yoga is a form of hygiene, it is as useful to [Western man] as any other system. In the deepest sense, however, yoga does not mean this but, if I understand it correctly, a great deal more, namely the final release and detachment of consciousness from all bondage to object and subject. But since one cannot detach oneself from something of which one is unconscious, the European must first learn to know his subject. This, in the West, is what one calls the unconscious. Yoga technique applies itself exclusively to the conscious mind and will. Such an undertaking promises success only when the unconscious has no potential worth mentioning, that is to say, when it does not contain large portions of the personality. If it does, then all conscious effort remains futile, and what comes out of this cramped condition of mind is a caricature or even the exact opposite of the intended result.[30]

---

[29] "Yoga and the West, *Psychology and Religion,* CW 11, par. 868.
[30] Ibid., par. 871.

I guess it is clear by now that in explicating Jung's work I tend to debouche into autobiography. This is not usual for writers in this genre, but it comes naturally to me and moreover is, I think, in tune with the classical ideal of salting weighty matters with bathos (or is it pathos?), and Jung's view that one's personal psychology and experience unavoidably inform one's outlook on life,[31] much as in scientific experiments the role of the observer cannot be discounted.

Jung himself, of course, though not chary about his psychological views, was parsimonious in revealing details of his personal life. He cleverly sidestepped the inevitable interest of others by declaiming in the prologue to his autobiography:

> I early arrived at the insight that when no answer comes from within to the problems and complexities of life, they ultimately mean very little. Outward circumstances are no substitute for inner experience. Therefore my life has been singularly poor in outward happenings. I cannot tell much about them, for it would strike me as hollow and insubstantial. I can understand myself only in the light of inner happenings. It is these that make up the singularity of my life, and with these my autobiography deals.[32]

Well, clearly spoken by a true introverted intuitive, the type of person for whom the unconscious is more than an airy concept but rather an everyday companion.[33] Such people also have readier access to the transcendent than those not so psychologically endowed; the latter including myself, constantly dealing with sensation details that don't amount to a hill of

---

[31] See "Freud and Jung: Contrasts," *Jung Uncorked,* Book 3, pp. 43ff.

[32] *Memories, Dreams, Reflections,* p. 5.

[33] See my *Personality Types,* pp. 84ff.

beans in the grand scheme of things, but at least make life worth living day by day in the here and now.

Okay, enough of that. What is "Yoga and the West" all about? For a start, I can note, as the editors of this volume point out, that "Jung was struck by the contrasting methods of observation employed by religious men of the East and by those of the predominantly Christian West."[34]

It is a short essay, a dozen pages easily read in about fifteen minutes, though its substance can take a few hours, even years, to digest. In the first half Jung outlines the slow decline, in Europe, in religious faith since the fifteenth-century Renaissance, coupled with a growing belief in scientific knowledge as humanity's salvation. This led to a split in the Western mind between science and philosophy (religion, metaphysics, etc.). This movement was hastened by the rise of Protestantism with its hundreds of sects intent on attacking the authority of the Roman Catholic Church as "the indispensable agent of divine salvation":

> Thus the burden of authority fell to the individual, and with it a religious responsibility that had never existed before. The decline of confession and absolution sharpened the moral conflict of the individual and burdened him with problems which previously the Church had settled for him, since her sacraments, particularly that of the Mass, guaranteed his salvation through the priest's enactment of the sacred rite. The only things the individual had to contribute were confession, repentance, and penance. With the collapse of the rite, which did the work for him, he had to do without God's answer to his plans. This dissatisfaction explains the demand for systems

---

[34] "Editorial Note," *Psychology and Religion,* CW 11, p. v.

that promise an answer—the visible or at least noticeable favour of another (higher, spiritual, or divine) power.[35]

Meanwhile, in the later nineteenth century, with the translation of the *Upanishads,* there developed an interest in Eastern, particularly Indian, philosophy and religious practices such as yoga. Some attempts were made to combine traditional religious beliefs with a scientific attitude (Christian Science, theosophy, anthroposophy, for instance), but these were fringe movements at best. Yoga, however, did gain a foothold, attracting many adherents in search of enlightenment, and today is more popular than ever. Nevertheless, Jung throws cold water on its spiritual efficacy for Westerners:

> In the East, where these ideas and practices originated, and where an uninterrupted tradition extending over some four thousand years has created the necessary spiritual conditions, yoga is, as I can readily believe, the perfect and appropriate method of fusing body and mind together so that they form a unity that can hardly be doubted. They thus create a psychological disposition which makes possible intuitions that transcend consciousness. . . . The West, on the contrary, with its bad habit of wanting to believe on the one hand, and its highly developed scientific and philosophical critique on the other, finds itself in a real dilemma. Either it falls into the trap of faith and swallows concepts like *prana, atman, chakra, samadhi,* etc., without giving them a thought, or its scientific critique repudiates them . . . as "pure mysticism." The split in the Western mind therefore makes it impossible at the outset for the intentions of yoga to be realized in any adequate way.[36]

---

[35] "Yoga and the West," ibid., par. 867.

[36] Ibid., par. 866.

Personally, I was curious enough about yoga to take lessons—and I tried Pilates too—at the local health club for a couple of years until they bored me out of my skull. Along with the other few men in the class I developed a crush on the nubile lycra-clad nymphet instructor, but alas the age difference worked against pursuing a social relationship.

Earlier, when I lived in Zurich, I also did some yoga. It didn't take with me then either, but I was more successful in bedding the winsome teacher Sylvine, who by day was an antique dealer on the Niederdorf (shadowy Lower Town). She gave me a good price on a two-hundred-year-old gold snake ring when I received my diploma from the Jung Institute and packed my bags to return, regretfully, to Toronto. I hated to leave Switzerland, but I was ready to brave the North American ethic with the psychological tools I had acquired to change the world. It is the end stage of the hero's journey, after all, a time when he is obliged, archetypally speaking, to impart to his contemporaries the presumed wisdom and insights garnered on his journey into self.[37] And that was what I immodestly intended to do, have done, and will continue doing, *Deo concedente* (God willing).

By the way, Sylvine visited me in Toronto but it didn't work out so well. The only thing we had in common was that we were so different.

Oh, I almost forgot the yoga camp I went to on Paradise Island in Nassau for a couple of summers running. Then I was coupled with a serious adept who rose from our intimate antics in a tent to greet the sun with the exhausting "breath of

---

[37] See my *Jung Lexicon*, pp. 59ff.

fire." But that is another story, best left for my elusive novel and Ruth Gordon in the incomparably charming 1970s' film *Harold and Maude.*

All in all, yoga was definitely not for me. I could just about get my heart and head around the philosophy behind it, but not the kinesiology, which seemed to me to be about bending your body into terrifically painful positions intended to cut off the flow of blood to your skeptical brain. I finally had to give it up, and stole away from the health club several hundred dollars poorer with only an uncomfortable purple rubber body mat half an inch thick.

The above experiences lead me to agree with Jung's final declaration in this essay that yoga as a spiritual discipline is not appropriate for Western folks, more likely to be distracting than enlightening. He puts his faith instead in depth analysis and the practice of active imagination,[38] disciplines designed to reveal unconscious contents rather than ignore or obscure them. We simply do not have the centuries-old cultural background for a physical and mental discipline that aims at the obliteration of the conscious mind and the embracing of esoteric Eastern concepts like *pranayama* that are even less digestible than my dear gramma's rice pudding.

I am not, however, against yoga practice by others who find it relaxing or enlivening. I have several clients who swear by it, especially when combined with meditation on soul-values. I am not judgmental regarding such matters when they are in accord with a person's individuation rather than an escape from it, which is always the hard-to-assess "bottom line."

---

[38] See *Jung Uncorked,* Book One, pp. 95ff.

Indeed, one of Inner City Books' analyst authors, Judith Harris, herself a professional yoga teacher, writes eloquently and convincingly of her experience:

> For many years I sought a form of bodywork that I could incorporate into my daily life. . . . Yoga appealed to me as a possible path for bringing spirit into body in a balanced, conscious way. And so, my initiation into bodywork began.
>
> Suddenly, I was faced with all my fears and inferiorities. Just to remain present for ninety minutes challenged me to the core of my being. . . . I began to feel what it was like to be *in* my body for the first time. . . .
>
> Many of us have endured a life not-yet-lived. In this mysterious place between the opposites, we may finally find our own life. There, previously hidden energy brings psyche and body together, uniting them in the sacred union that gives birth to new consciousness, and the gift of a life fully lived.[39]

All the same, Jung's last paragraph in "Yoga and the West" is worth quoting in its entirety:

> If I remain so critically averse to yoga, it does not mean that I do not regard this spiritual achievement of the East as one of the greatest things the human mind has ever created. I hope my exposition makes it sufficiently clear that my criticism is directed solely against the application of yoga to the peoples of the West. The spiritual development of the West has been along entirely different lines from that of the East and has therefore produced conditions which are the most unfavourable soil one can think of for the application of yoga. Western civilization is scarcely a thousand years old and must first of

---

[39] *Jung and Yoga: The Psyche-Body Connection,* p. 9.

all free itself from its barbarous one-sidedness. This means, above all, deeper insight into the nature of man. But no insight is gained by repressing and controlling the unconscious, and least of all by imitating methods which have grown up under totally different psychological conditions. In the course of the centuries the West will produce its own yoga, and it will be on the basis laid down by Christianity.[40]

Well, that's a powerful mouthful. How about a song now? While working on this chapter I have been listening to Ms. Black Velvet, Nina Simone. The following is one of my favorites. It is a far cry from yoga, but please, leave me to my devices:

> I take
> Just like a woman
> Yes I do
> And I make love
> just like a woman
> and I ache
> just like a woman
> but I break
> like a little girl
>
> Nobody here feels any pain
> tonight as I stand inside the rain
> And no one has to guess
> that baby's got new clothes
> Lately I see her ribbons and her bows
> and the problems
> from her curls
>
> I take
> just like a woman. . .

---

[40] "Yoga and the West," *Psychology and Religion,* CW 10, par. 876.

It was raining from the first
and I was dying here of thirst
That's why I came here
and a long time's curse
and what's worse
is this pain in here
I can't stay in here
Ain't it clear
Ain't it clear
I must admit
I believe it's time for me to quit
And until we meet again
Bein' introduced as friends
please don't let on
that you knew me when
I was hungry
and it was your world . . .

I take just like a woman. . . .[41]

And I give, just like a man.

``````````````

---

[41] "Just Like a Woman," from *Nina Simone: Love Songs;* lyrics by Bob Dylan; BMG Music.
``````````````

12
Religious Ideas in Alchemy
(from *Psychology and Alchemy,* CW 12, vintage 1944/1952)

To move from yoga to alchemy was for Jung as natural and simple as crossing the street in a familiar town. Not so for the modern lay reader, including myself, who can easily get lost in the labyrinthine, overlapping twists of Jung's interests. It helps, I think, to know how he introduces this volume:

> Some thirty-five years ago I noticed to my amazement that European and American men and women coming to me for psychological advice were producing in their dreams and fantasies symbols similar to, and often identical with, the symbols found in the mystery religions of antiquity, in mythology, folklore, fairytales, and the apparently meaningless formulations of such esoteric cults as alchemy. Experience showed, moreover, that these symbols brought with them new energy and new life to the people to whom they came.
>
> From long and careful comparison and analysis of these products of the unconscious I was led to postulate a "collective unconscious," a source of energy and insight in the depth of the human psyche which has operated in and through man from the earliest periods of which we have records.[42]

There, in something more than a nutshell, we have the genesis of Jung's school of analytical psychology. He went far beyond Freud in seeing, and presenting evidence of, a layer of the human psyche

---

[42] "Prefatory Note to the English Edition," *Psychology and Alchemy,* CW 12, p. v.

that was other than personal—a layer he called the objective, collective or archetypal unconscious.

Only now, some fifty years after Jung's death, is the significance of this discovery beginning to sink in and take hold of the popular imagination. However, even among the educated public and media there is still a good deal of confusion about the difference between "stereotypical" and "archetypal." In short, the former refers to a cultural image of a person or thing that is typical and ubiquitous (as in my earlier description of my mother as a stereotypical mid-twentieth-century housewife, or myself as a struggling writer). "Archetypal," however, refers to a primordial, structural element of the human psyche that manifests in a particular pattern of behavior that is unconsciously determined and more or less beyond conscious apprehension and control. Granted, the distinction is confusing. For example, an older man who behaves in an adolescent manner may be stereotypical (that is, similar to others), but underlying his way of functioning is the archetype of the *puer aeternus* (eternal child). A stereotypical housewife, too, might be said to be acting out an archetype, but that would depend on many individual factors beyond the scope of this discourse.

It took me almost two hours to write the preceding paragraph; that's how taxed I am to understand and articulate these concepts. So you will forgive me, I hope, for taking a break and interjecting a love song from the "lady of the gardenias," Billie Holiday.

> I fell in love with you first time I looked into
> Them there eyes
> You've got a certain li'l cute way of flirtin' with
> Them there eyes
> They make me feel happy
> They make me feel blue

No stallin'
I'm fallin'
Going in a big way for sweet little you
My heart is jumpin'
Sure started somethin' with
Them there eyes
You'd better watch them if you're wise
They sparkle
They bubble
They're gonna get you in a whole lot of trouble
You're overworkin' them
There's danger lurkin' in
Them there eyes
Maybe you think I'm just flirtin'
Maybe you think I'm all lies
Just because I get romantic when I gaze in
Them there eyes.[43]

You may wonder what Ms. Holiday has to do with religious ideas in alchemy. Well, I do too. But apparently I am having difficulty getting into this essay.

Yet, my problem is surely a cakewalk compared to what Jung did. Imagine plowing through all those arcane medieval manuscripts in Latin and Greek, even with the help of the classical scholar Marie-Louise von Franz, to get to the heart of the alchemical quest. Curiously, perhaps, Jung did not become erotically involved with Dr. von Franz (though it is likely, I think, that the real working alchemist and his *soror mystica* hit the hay together after toying with alembics and their projected unconscious). Jung chose

---

[43] From *Billie Holiday's Greatest Hits;* words and music by Maceo Pinkard, William Tracey and Doris Tauber; ASCAP.

instead the wispy Toni Wolff, by all accounts an intuitive dynamo in her own right and a little closer to his own age.[44]

The motivation for all Jung's investigations into the mystery of alchemy was that he discerned its psychic nature. From that base he teased out its religious significance. This was and is no small feat. According to many websites on the Internet, there are moderns who still believe that alchemical procedures were aimed at producing gold from lead, and these benighted folks continue to experiment with secret recipes in their high-tech laboratories.[45] No doubt there are also those who believe the moon is made of blue cheese, in spite of mineral samples brought back to earth by astronauts. And the Flat-Earth Society? Don't get me started.

Recall Jung's definition of religion as the careful observation and consideration of irrational factors. The medieval mind was swept up by and thrived on the irrational. Not so different from the modern Christian fundamentalist who cannot see the symbolic nature of the Gospels. Jung saw through the mystifying array of chemicals and procedures to the heart of the enterprise, namely an attempt at self-understanding, analogous to what we now call the process of individuation. Edward F. Edinger explains why this is so useful to the modern individual:

> The great value of alchemical images is that they give us an *objective* basis from which to approach dreams and other unconscious material. With the psyche more than with any other subject it is very difficult to distinguish between objective fact and personal bias. A working knowledge of alchemical images can be very help-

---

[44] Much of this is wonderfully documented with feeling and discretion in Barbara Hannah, *Jung: His Life and Work (A Personal Memoir)*. Consider also Ms. Wolff's seminal work, *Structural Forms of the Feminine Psyche.*

[45] Google it yourself: "alchemical experiments"—8,130 hits, July 20, 2008.

ful in promoting this much-needed objectivity. Our goal, given suf-ficient familiarity with archetypal symbolism and sufficient self-knowledge from personal analysis, is an anatomy of the psyche that is as objective as the anatomy of the body.[46]

To this I cannot forebear adding the following remarks by the late Marie-Louise von Franz, Jung's foremost disciple:

[Jung] himself discovered alchemy absolutely empirically. He once told me that he frequently came across certain motifs in his pa-tients' dreams which he could not understand, and then one day he started to look at old books on alchemy and noticed a connection. For example, a woman patient dreamt that an eagle was at first fly-ing up to the sky, and then suddenly, turning round its head, began to eat its own wings and dropped back onto the earth. Dr. Jung was naturally able to understand this symbolism without historical par-allels—the high soaring spirit, or thought bird, so to speak. The dream indicates a sort of enantiodromia, the reversal of a psychic situation. All the same, he was very much struck by the motif which one at once recognizes as archetypal and which one feels convinced must have parallels; it strikes one as a general motif, yet it was no-where to be found. Then one day he discovered the Ripley Scroll, which gives a series of pictures of the alchemical process—partly published in *Psychology and Alchemy*—where there is an eagle with a king's head, which turns back and eats its own wings.[47]

My explication here is lamentably brief, I know, but I have al-ready mined this lode substantially in an earlier book in this se-ries,[48] and I am always on the verge of repeating myself.

---

[46] *Anatomy of the Psyche: Alchemical Symbolism in Psychotherapy,* p. xix.

[47] *Alchemy: An Introduction to the Symbolism and the Psychology,* p. 14.

[48] See "The Psychic Nature of the Alchemical Work," *Jung Uncorked,* Book Two, chap. 12, pp. 45ff., and ibid., pp. 59ff.

That is true too in the area of romance, where I have no excuse but the sheer fun of it. How about this stunner by Tina Turner:

I found a friend, someone to help me
And a place I can be myself when I'm in trouble now
I've lost it and I don't know how
I come to you 'cause you can show me
Get me back to the me I know with a remedy
Baby I need your therapy
With your healing kiss you know how to make my mind relax
I will listen to the words you say and just lie back
Talk to my heart that's where real talkin' starts
Words of love that cut straight to my heart
Reach out and touch, so few words say so much
I can hear you when you tell it like it is
When you talk straight to my heart
I guess it shows I need attention
Somehow you're asking all the right questions that I've gotta say
What's been on my mind these days
And I know you know just how to make my mind react
When it's coming straight from you that's my first point of contact
Talk to my heart that's where real talkin' starts
Words of love that cut straight to my heart
Reach out and touch, so few words say so much
I can hear you when you tell it like it is
When you talk straight to my. . . .
I'm bad at making decisions
But being alone with you just feels so right, feels so right
I'm losing my inhibitions
With every minute I share with you tonight, share with you tonight
Talk, talk to me
To my heart, to my heart, oh yeah
Come on, come on and reach out

'Cause the words just mean so much
I can hear you
When you talk right to my heart
Talk to my heart that's where real talkin' starts
Words of love that cut straight to my heart
Reach out and touch, so few words say so much
I can hear you when you tell it like it is
When you talk straight to my heart.[49]

Straight talk to the heart is soul-talk, quite as rare as rainbows and as much of a covenant as the "bow" shown to Noah by the Lord after the Flood.[50]

---

[49] "Talk to My Heart," from *Tina: Twenty Four Seven;* lyrics by Johhny Douglas and Graham Lyle; ASCAP.

[50] Gen. 9:13.

13
The Philosophical Tree
(from *Alchemical Studies,* CW 14, vintage 1945/1954)

An image which frequently appears among the archetypal configurations of the unconscious is that of the tree or the wonder-working plant. When these fantasy products are drawn or painted, they very often fall into symmetrical patterns that take the form of a mandala. If a mandala may be described as a symbol of the self seen in cross section, then the tree would represent a profile view of it: the self depicted as a process of growth. . . . The examples I now propose to give all come from a series of pictures in which my patients tried to express their inner experiences.

. . . . My case material has not been influenced in any way, for none of the patients had any previous knowledge of alchemy or of shamanism. The pictures were spontaneous products of creative fantasy, and their only conscious purpose was to express what happens when unconscious contents are taken over into consciousness in such a way that it is not overwhelmed by them and the unconscious not subjected to any distortion. Most of the pictures were done by patients who were under treatment, but some by persons who were not, or were no longer, under therapeutic influence. I must emphasize that I carefully avoided saying anything in advance that might have had a suggestive effect. Nineteen of the thirty-two pictures were done at a time when I myself knew nothing of alchemy.[51]

---

[51] "The Philosophical Tree," *Alchemical Studies,* CW 13, pars. 304f.

Following this disclaimer or caveat, as it were, Jung presents the thirty-two images of the tree as it surfaced in the material of his contemporaries.

Space forbids reproducing these pictures here, but it must be said that Jung's depth interpretations mark a milestone in the scientific, empirical investigation of products of the unconscious. This yeoman task had not previously been undertaken.

The extraordinary variety of the depictions is remarkable in itself. There are trees breaking through the earth's crust; trees in flame; trees without leaves; trees threatened by dragons or crocodiles; protected by serpents; fruitless or heavy-laden with bounty. In some there is a key in the roots and birds in the branches guarding the treasure. A tree stands in isolation, carries a nymph, or its roots mother a sleeping human figure undergoing metamorphosis like the larva of an insect.

I was awestruck at the psychological dimensions of this image explored by Jung, which was otherwise, in my experience, simply a gnarled collection of branches outside my window limiting my view onto the street. Pity the blindness of the non-intuitive.

Jung comments on the traditional maternal significance of the tree and the generally benign nature of it as an archetypal image in dreams and other unconscious material. He explains at length:

> Although it will be obvious to anyone acquainted with the material that my examples are nothing more than special instances of a widely disseminated tree symbolism, it is nevertheless of importance, in interpreting the individual symbols, to know something about their historical antecedents. Like all

archetypal symbols, the symbol of the tree has undergone a development of meaning in the course of the centuries. It is far removed from the original meaning of the shamanistic tree, even though certain basic features prove to be unalterable. The psychoid form underlying any archetypal image retains its character at all stages of development, though empirically it is capable of endless variations. The outward form of the tree may change in the course of time, but the richness and vitality of a symbol are expressed more in its change of meaning. The aspect of meaning is therefore essential to the phenomenology of the tree symbol. Taken on average, the commonest associations to its meaning are growth, life, unfolding of form in a physical and spiritual sense, development, growth from below upwards and from above downwards, the maternal aspect (protection, shade, shelter, nourishing fruits, source of life, solidity, permanence, firm-rootedness, but also being "rooted to the spot"), old age, personality, and finally death and rebirth.[52]

This is such a comprehensive assessment of tree symbolism that I cannot immediately think of how to continue. How did I get out on this limb anyway? I need a break and some music, like this duet from *The Phantom of the Opera:*

> [Michael Crawford:]
> Nighttime sharpens,
> Heightens each sensation . . .
> Darkness stirs and wakes imagination.
> Silently the senses abandon their defenses
> Helpless to resist the notes I write
> For I composed the music of the night!
>
> [Barbra Streisand:]

---

[52] Ibid., par. 350. The wider symbolism of the garden is explored in Margaret Eileen Meredith, *The Secret Garden: Temenos for Individuation.*

Slowly, gently
Night unfurls its splendor.
Grasp it, sense it tremulous and tender.

[Both:]
Hearing is believing, music is deceiving,
Hard as lightning, soft as candle light,

[Michael:]
There you trust the music of the night. . . .

[Barbra:]
Close your eyes,
For your eyes will only tell the truth,

[Both:]
And the truth isn't what you want to see.
In the dark it is easy to pretend
That the truth is what it ought to be. . . .

[Michael:]
Softly,

[Barbra:]
Deafening,

[Both:]
Music shall caress you.

[Barbra:]
Hear it,

[Michael:]
Feel it,

[Both:]
Secretly possess you. . . .
Open up your mind, let your fantasies unwind,
In this darkness which you know you cannot fight,
The darkness of the music of the night. . . .
Close your eyes start a journey through a strange new world
Leave all thoughts of the world you knew before!
Close your eyes and let music set you free!

Only then can you belong to me. . . .
Floating (floating), falling (falling)
Sweet intoxication!
Touch me (touch me), trust me (trust me)
Savor each sensation!
Let the dream begin,
Let your darker side give in
To the power of the music that I write,
The power of the music of the night.[53]

Okay, now I think of a long-ago client I shall call Daisy, because she cultivated a rooftop flowerbed. Her situation was not unusual. She was fifty-something, had a teen-age son and was married to a stockbroker, happily, except he did not take her as seriously as she did herself. Their intimacy was perfunctory, their sex life minimal. Her initial presenting conflict was her attraction to a neighbor who was wont to hose her down when watering his lawn. He was not otherwise flirtatious, but Daisy had fantasies; she wondered if she might, or ought to, take the initiative. She was tied up in knots about this, for she had been brought up as a Catholic and her marriage vows were sacrosanct.

Jiminy Cricket! I felt for her. I saw it as an archetypal situation, and not one to take lightly when it manifests as a suffering woman in front of you seeking counsel.

I did little more than usual. I listened, supported her vacillations, and encouraged her to keep track of her dreams. Daisy was a very attractive woman and I became a little in love with her. That always helps in my profession, for without Eros

[53] "Music of the Night," from *Barbra Streisand: Greatest Hits/* ASCAP.

there is only the darkness of the night, and no music.

Over many months, Daisy came to realize that she had an inner man whom she had projected onto her hoser neighbor, who by later accounts—including clothesline gossip with his wife—was simply a playful jock more interested in football and squash than anyone's pudendum. This put paid to Daisy's longing for a literally meaningful phallic encounter, though it left her rather high and dry. But not for too long. At the height of her despair, she dreamed:

> I am a tree. I have branches and blossoms. Birds sit in me and sing. Squirrels go up and down my limbs. My leaves seek the sun and my roots swim in water.

Our dialogue around this dream took us far afield, eventually uncovering her hitherto unexpressed desire for more education, which she subsequently and happily undertook.

One might say that Daisy had been unconsciously seeking a creative outlet for her frustrated energies—previously historically, culturally, and by her, associated with an outer man. In her work on herself, she discovered and dialogued with her inner man, her animus, her own phallic/creative energies.

I was there and applauded when she received a degree in computer science. By then she had left her husband and had a new relationship, no more or less problematic than any other—but she at least had some psychological tools with which to weather the inevitable storms.

It is very challenging, being an analyst or therapist of any kind. Of course, the stevedore, the stenographer, the plumber, the CEO and crane operator have their woes, but they aren't usually involved with the souls of others. In the so-called helping professions, we cannot avoid soul-work, at whatever depth. We may peripherally influence behavior patterns, but our real focus is on the essential, core personality, so elusive to identify and yet so satisfying to see develop.

Here's a dandy to bring back memories:

> Here comes the sun
> Here comes the sun, here comes the sun,
> and I say it's all right
>
> Little darling, it's been a long cold lonely winter
> Little darling, it feels like years since it's been here
> Here comes the sun, here comes the sun
> and I say it's all right
>
> Little darling, the smiles returning to the faces
> Little darling, it seems like years since it's been here
> Here comes the sun, here comes the sun
> and I say it's all right
>
> Sun, sun, sun, here it comes. . . .
>
> Little darling, I feel that ice is slowly melting
> Little darling, it seems like years since it's been clear
> Here comes the sun, here comes the sun,
> and I say it's all right
> It's all right.[54]

That is hard to beat for optimism, whether in or out of a relationship, and I'm all for it. Call me a child of the 1960s, I got nothing to lose but sleep.

---

[54] "Here Comes the Sun," *The Beatles,* written by George Harrison; ASCAP.

14
The Components of the Coniunctio
(from *Mysterium Coniunctionis,* CW 14, vintage 1954)

The factors which come together in the coniunctio are conceived as opposites, either confronting one another in enmity
or attracting one another in love. To begin with they form a
dualism . . . . Often the polarity is arranged as a quaternio
(quaternity), with the two opposites crossing one another, as
for instance the four elements or the four qualities (moist, dry,
cold, warm), or the four directions and seasons, thus producing the cross as an emblem of the four elements and symbol of
the sublunary physical world.[55]

I am sorely tempted here to resurrect Ms. Cotton Pants, the
pneumatic young lady I plucked from obscurity earlier in this
series.[56] She has been much on my mind as I re-read this section of Jung's major work on alchemy. My interest is not pru-
rient, but rather pragmatic, and so I will not resist her re-
appearance.
    You may recall that I used her personable antics meta-
phorically, anecdotally, archetypally, in explicating the significance of Mercurius in the alchemical *opus.* It is true that
some readers found it crude and tasteless, but others conceded
it to be appropriate for the context, albeit somewhat risqué for
a book of a purported serious nature.

---

[55] "The Components of the Coniunctio," *Mysterium Coniunctionis,* CW 14, par. 1.
[56] See *Jung Uncorked,* Book Two, pp. 63f, 69f.

One irate reader said I should be defrocked. A friend counterpunched: "Better to have loved and been defrocked than never to have frocked at all." Which put me in mind of Jung's admonition: "If you don't live your nonsense you will never have lived at all, and the meaning of life is surely that it is lived, not avoided."[57] Anyway, the Jungian community doesn't defrock analysts, just condemns them to reading their own books over and over and over.

Be that as it may, since Ms. Cotton Pants' induction into the Nobel hall of fame for her mature work on schizophrenia we have spent many a pleasant soirée together playing backgammon or discussing the nature of the *pleroma,* which for her is like playing chess with a toad.

Pragmatically, any coniunctio requires a vis-à-vis, a partner. More, a willing participant in the dance of the senses, or alternatively, as in my loverNot relationship with Cottie (as I have come to call her), an appreciation of the bizarre and absurd, as evidenced for instance in my book *Chicken Little: The Inside Story,* featuring Professor Adam Brillig, which Cottie found enchanting, intriguing, and an adventure worthy of Indiana Jones. I know this because her doctoral thesis, "The Barnyard as a Source of *Concupiscence*," quoted generously from my own forays into the fowl psyche. Indeed, I only dissuaded her from becoming a card-carrying Chickle-Schticker on the basis of her precarious academic situation, where misogynous colleagues are ever on the lookout for aberrant impulses on the part of female faculty.[58]

---

[57] *Visions: Notes of the Seminar Given in 1930-1934,* p. 1147.

[58] Chickle-Schtick is the area of academic research that focuses on fears of the end of the world, exemplified by Chicken Little's dire warning that the sky is falling.

As noted above, Ms. Cotton Pants, in her ascension to the airy heights of academe, did not forsake her earthy background or supportive friends such as myself. Thus I trust she will not mind if I divulge one of her favorite tunes from the sixties, when she was deeply involved in the peace movement and alternative lifestyles:

> Slow down, you're moving too fast,
> you got to make the morning last,
> just kicking down the cobblestones,
> looking for fun and feeling groovy.
>
> *Ba da da da da da da,* feeling groovy.
>
> Hello lamppost, whatcha knowing?
> I've come to watch your flowers growing.
> Ain't ya got no rhymes for me?
>
> *Doo doo doo doo,* feeling groovy.
> *Ba da da da da da da,* feeling groovy.
>
> I got no deeds to do, no promises to keep.
> I'm dappled and drowsy and ready to sleep.
> Let the morning time drop all its petals on me,
> Life I love you, all is groovy.
> *Doo doo doo doo,* feeling groovy.[59]

To be fair, Cottie sometimes seems a little piqued when at the end of an intimately imaginative evening playing scrabble, say, or listening to Beethoven or Sarah Vaughan, I debouche to my separate sleeping quarters, but she is not forward and does not force the issue. Truth to tell, I often wish she would, for a lone coniunctio is a sad oxymoron, a pale shadow of the real thing. I do desire her, and I am hopelessly in love with the image of her in my head, but I respect her attachment to

---

[59] Simon and Garfunkle, "The 59th Street Bridge Song (Feelin Groovy)"; ASCAP.

her husband, the esteemed Professor Emmanuel Flatbush, head of the department of endocrinology at the University of Toronto, and anyway she is really too smart for me.

Now, all the above, of course, is speaking intrapsychically, which most assuredly is what this introductory section of *Mysterium Coniunctionis* is all about, no matter where the thoughts of red-blooded men and women may roam. Whatever libidinous hijinks the *artifex* (alchemist) and his *soror mystica* may have got up to outside the laboratory, their quest in the workplace, as Jung saw it, was both literal and symbolic and attuned to self-understanding, whether they knew it or not. Some may indeed have envisioned the end-product of their labors, the vaunted *lapis,* a.k.a. *filius philosophorum* or Philosophers' Stone, literally as hunks of gold transmuted from lead, which perhaps accounts for their attempts to mystify brigands with incomprehensible nomenclature. But the more thoughtful practitioners whose manuscripts have survived and whose names have come down to us—Michael Maier, Gerhard Dorn, Stolcenberg, Mylius, Ripley, Lambspringk, etc.—arguably knew what they were doing, however obfuscated in their written descriptions.

The representation of the opposites in alchemical tracts is legion, ranging from elemental or cosmic antimonies like fire and water, earth and air, life and death, to theriomorphic images such as winged and wingless birds or dragons, eagle and toad, two fishes, stag and unicorn. But it is not mere whimsy, I think, that the opposites were most often represented as Sol and Luna or king and queen, for asexual, genderless images have never been as potent in primitive ritual or incantatory rites as those symbolizing the coupling of the sexes. Well, modern advertisers of everything from soap to cars have long known it, and even the Roman Catholic Church takes advantage of that association, however covertly, in the Mass.

In alchemical lore, the *prima materia* (original matter) was concretely the base metal lead, which had to undergo various transformations in a *pelikan* (glass retort) under strict conditions, on its way to becoming gold. Jung saw this for what it meant psychologically. Thus in depth analysis the *prima materia* refers to both the instinctual foundation of life and the raw, everyday material one has to work with—dreams, emotions, conflicts, etc. Mayhap the client's entire life and range of attitudes come under the microscope in an effort to uncover the often surprising *terma*—a Buddhist concept referring to a treasure that has been buried and remains buried until such time as it is needed and found . . . like a sacred script or a Bodhisatva.[60]

The first stage in the alchemist's alembic was to apprehend the *nigredo,* the darkness, seen as impurities that needed to be distilled out in order to move on. Psychologically, the *nigredo* corresponds to the mental disorientation that typically arises in the process of assimilating unconscious contents, particularly aspects of the shadow. Jung says it very well in a later section of this volume:

> Self-knowledge is an adventure that carries us unexpectedly far and deep. Even a moderately comprehensive knowledge of the shadow can cause a good deal of confusion and mental darkness, since it gives rise to personality problems which one had never remotely imagined before. For this reason alone we

---

[60] I am grateful to John Robert Colombo, dean of quotable quotes, for this allusion.

can understand why the alchemists called their *nigredo* melancholia, "a black blacker than black," night, an affliction of the soul, confusion, etc., or, more pointedly, the "black raven." For us the raven seems only a funny allegory, but for the medieval adept it was . . . a well-known allegory of the devil.[61]

The literal alchemist, after surviving the despair inherent in the *nigredo,* moved on to the next stage.

Okay, let us take a case in point—my fantasy relationship with Ms. Cotton Pants or her anima image. The first step would be to differentiate my shadowy desire *(nigredo)*—shadowy because morally aberrant—from the realistic possibilities and the potential consequences of acting it out. That might take a year or two.

The next step in the alchemical canon, the *albedo* (whitening), has to do with the integration of complexes and their projection, particularly the contrasexual anima/animus, those undercover movers of heaven and earth. This work is long and exhausting, sometimes activating what the alchemists called the "madness of the lead," a state of mind in which life itself may seem meaningless. For most of us, this is temporary, but some people do jump off bridges or harm others when *in extremis.* In the *albedo* phase, it can take two to three years at the very least to know what's what.

After an extended time of such self-examination, one may come to the alchemical reddening or *rubedo,* which is a state where the ego realizes its powerlessness relative to the Self, the central organizing principle in the psyche, whose plans for us, so to speak, do not necessarily coincide with our ego-

---

[61] "The Conjunction," *Mysterium Coniunctionis,* CW 14, par. 741.

desires. This guiding principle is God by another name, though not outside but within. This is a goal (gold), the treasure hard to attain, seldom reached in a lifetime.

Finally, then, when I have capped my lust for the numinous Ms. Cotton Pants, I can content myself with the happy affection accorded me by my real-life paramour (MP), who is more than a passing fancy in my harem.

The components of the coniunctio, however arcanely they were named, are essentially masculine and feminine, with all that entails in the conflicts and compromises experienced in any human relationship. Listen to that charmer, Rod Stewart, plucking our hearts:

> It must have been Moonglow,
> Way up in the blue,
> It must have been Moonglow,
> That led me straight to you
> I still hear you sayin'
> Dear one hold me fast,
> And I start to prayin'
> Oh Lord, please let this last,
> We seem to float right through the air,
> Heavenly songs seem to come from everywhere,
> And now when there's Moonglow,
> Way up in the blue,
> I always remember,
> That Moonglow gave me you
> That Moonglow gave me you.[62]

Pardon me. I am inclined to slip-slide into flights of fancy

---

[62] "Moonglow," from "It Had To Be You," in *The Great American Songbook;* music and lyrics by Gus Kahn and Isham Jones; ASCAP.

in the deep of the night. I wish Ms. Cotton Pants were real and here. I could suggest a simple dalliance, just for the fun of it, but at her stage of life and wisdom—go on with ya, any woman of any age—no dalliance is simple; love-making involves the intertwining of lips and limbs, the commingling of body and soul, and there is no getting around it mamby-pamby by imagining it to be merely a mechanical, objective act or a coupling of convenience. Complexes assert themselves, loving feelings erupt, projections flourish, not to mention the ongoing, unconscious animus/anima dialogue. And, of course, Ms. Cotton Pants would be understandably wary, as would I, considering my long-standing attachment to MP. Conflict galore! Anyway, in the real world I don't have the time or energy for more than one paramour.

So call my impulse the madness of the lead or midnight madness, it comes to the same thing: solitude longing for coniunctio, and better taken symbolically than acted out, in spite of Grace Slick belting it out at Woodstock 1969:

> When the truth is found to be lies
> and all the joy within you dies
> don't you want somebody to love
> don't you need somebody to love
> wouldn't you love somebody to love
> you better find somebody to love
> When the garden flowers baby are dead yes
> and your mind [your mind] is [so] full of red
> don't you want somebody to love
> don't you need somebody to love
> wouldn't you love somebody to love
> you better find somebody to love
> your eyes, I say your eyes may look like his [yeah]

> but in your head baby I'm afraid you don't know where it is
> don't you want somebody to love
> don't you need somebody to love
> wouldn't you love somebody to love
> you better find somebody to love
> tears are running [ahhh,] running down your breast
> and your friends' baby they treat you like a guest.
> Don't you want somebody to love
> Don't you need somebody to love
> Wouldn't you love somebody to love
> you better find somebody to love.[63]

Okay, so what are the chances that Ms Cotton Pants and I will some day share a bed? That is an open question, but I'd say 60/40, odds in her favor. Bets will be held by Rachel, no prejudice.

I cannot leave this chapter without mentioning the adventurous medieval alchemist Michael Maier's unexpected encounter in Africa with the fabulously bizarre four-footed creature called the Ortus, which Maier encountered, notes Jung, in "that region of the psyche which was not unjustly said to be inhabited by, of all things, 'Pans, Satyrs, dog-headed baboons, and half-men,' "[64] and continues:

> It is not difficult to see that this region is the animal soul in man. For just as a man has a body which is no different in principle from that of an animal, so also his psychology has a whole series of lower storeys in which the spectres from humanity's past epochs still dwell, then the animal souls from

---

[63] "Somebody To Love," *Jefferson Airplane;* from www.lyircs007.com; ASCAP.

[64] "The Personification of the Opposites," *Mysterium Coniunctionis,* CW 14, par. 279.

the age of Pithecanthropus and the hominids, then the "psyche" of the cold-blooded saurians [lizards], and, deepest down of all, the transcendent mystery and paradox of the sympathetic and parasympathetic psychoid processes.[65]

One may dismiss this observation as chimerical, but the ubiquitous and powerful attraction between the sexes belies our skeptical denial of an animal soul more or less beyond our control. I tell you true, it is only my hair shirt that has stopped me from pouncing on a dozen barely-dressed maidens in the street over the past month (puer without pounce, another oxymoron).

I was overtaken this evening, possessed even, by *sol niger.* I opened *Jung Uncorked,* Book 2, in the middle (Ms. Cotton Pants) and couldn't stop reading until the end, all the time marveling at what a clever fella I was in the writing of it. "Look, Ma, no hands!" Who can top this, I often thought, for sheer wit and verve, modestly veiled self-revelation, academic yet earthy, illustrating the harmonious *coniunctio* of Logos and Eros? I fell deeply in love with it, unabashedly narcissistic and solipsistic. More: I could hardly recall the creation of it. It was as if I were admiring the work of a craftsman whose writing skills I aspired to. I even had to flip back to the cover to remind myself that it was truly I, or some semblance of me, who wrote it. This experience led me to reflect as follows.

People just gotta get it into their heads that the ego is not the be-all and end-all of their psychic life. For instance, although I would like to believe that the dazzling, vertiginous display of virtuosity evidenced in my writing—the clever

---

[65] Ibid.

melding of Logos and Eros, masculine and feminine, the suave, judicious leavening of the pure quill, etc.—is my sole ego-doing, sober second thoughts, and hints from my dreams, oblige me to concede that I bring to it only self-discipline, stamina and scotch, which three little sss's would count for naught without the collaboration of the one big S, the Self.

In the final analysis, we are all beholden to a Higher Power, whatever name we give it, in or outside of AA.

I cannot but play second fiddle to the Mystery; I am an instrument recording a dance/duet between consciousness and the unconscious, a sacred, ineffable relationship that I will dare to bring into the mundane with a *chanson à deux* between Barry Gibb and the playful Ms. Streisand:

[Barbra:]
Shadows falling, baby, we stand alone
Out on the street anybody you meet got a heartache of their own
(It oughta be illegal)
Make it a crime to be lonely or sad
(It oughta be illegal)
You got a reason for livin'
You battle on with the love you're livin' on
You gotta be mine
We take it away
It's gotta be night and day
Just a matter of time
And we got nothing to be guilty of
Our love will climb any mountain near or far , we are
And we never let it end
We are devotion
And we got nothing to be sorry for
Our love is one in a million

Eyes can see that we got a highway to the sky
I don't wanna hear your goodbye
Oh!

[Barry:]
Aaah!
Pulses racing , darling
How grand we are
Little by little we meet in the middle
There's danger in the dark
(It oughta be illegal)
Make it a crime to be out in the cold
(It oughta be illegal)
You got a reason for livin'
You battle on with the love you're buildin' on
Together
You gotta be mine
We take it away
It's gotta be night and day
Just a matter of time
And we got nothing to be guilty of
Our love will climb any mountain near or far , we are
And we never let it end
We are devotion
And we got nothing to be sorry for
Our love is one in a million
Eyes can see that we got a highway to the sky
And we got nothing to be guilty of. . . .[66]

Good night, Ms. Cotton Pants, Mrs. Flatbush, whoever you
are, wherever you be. It oughta be illegal to get tired just

---

[66] "Guilty," from *Barbra Streisand. Greatest Hits,* written by B. Gibb, R. Gibb, M. Gibb; ASCAP.

when you've built up a head of steam, but sleep beckons with the promise of renewed energy.

It is widely believed that older men seek the company of younger women. That may be statistically true, but not of me. Young lovelies engage my attention visually and instinctively, but I am more interested in relationships with older, mature women who have experienced life's storms and appreciate a safe port.

I think of a former client, an unmarried Anglican priest, who at the age of seventy-two confided to me his several affairs and said that he had never been happy without a lover.

Well, shite, who is? We are made to copulate, mayhap cohabit, and life without a mate to physically love is a fate relished only by Middle Ages' anchorites or modern hermetic monks and nuns who forsake human company in order to better praise their Lord without distractions of the flesh.

Not a life for me, bet your bottom dollar.

Maktub—it is written.

15
In Memory of Sigmund Freud
(from *The Spirit in Man, Art and Literature,* CW 15, vintage 1939)

I have chosen this essay from CW volume 15 because, though rather slim, it is an opportunity to consider the schism between Jung and his erstwhile mentor. Jung's "tribute," if it can be called such, begins like this:

> The cultural history of the past fifty years is inseparably bound up with the name of Sigmund Freud, the founder of psychoanalysis, who has just died. The Freudian outlook has affected practically every sphere of our contemporary thinking, except that of the exact sciences. Wherever the human psyche plays a decisive role, this outlook has left its mark, above all in the broad field of psychopathology, then in psychology, philosophy, aesthetics, ethnology and—last but not least—the psychology of religion. . . .
>
> Freud was first and foremost a "nerve specialist" in the strictest sense of this word, and in every respect he always remained one. By training he was no psychiatrist, no psychologist, and no philosopher. In philosophy he lacked even the most rudimentary elements of education. He once assured me personally that it had never occurred to him to read Nietzsche. This fact is of importance in understanding Freud's peculiar views, which are distinguished by an apparently total lack of any philosophical premises. His theories bear the unmistakable stamp of the doctor's consulting-room. His constant point of departure is the neurotically degenerate psyche, unfolding its secrets with a mixture of

reluctance and ill-concealed enjoyment under the critical eye of the doctor. But as the neurotic patient, besides having his individual sickness, is also an exponent of the local and contemporary mentality, a bridge exists from the start between the doctor's view of his particular case and certain general assumptions. The existence of this bridge enabled Freud to turn his intuition from the narrow confines of the consulting-room to the wide world of moral, philosophical, and religious ideas, which also, unhappily enough, proved themselves amenable to this critical investigation.[67]

One can easily see the ambivalence in Jung's appreciation—admiration tinged with sympathy for Freud's limitations, perhaps tainted by jealousy for Freud's fame, which had for the most part eluded Jung in the wider cultural arena. Nor must we forget that Freud's *Interpretation of Dreams* (1900) was the work that first sparked Jung's awareness of the importance of the unconscious. As Jung declares:

> For us young psychiatrists it was a fount of illumination, but for our older colleagues it was an object of mockery. As with his recognition that neurosis has the character of a medieval "possession," so, by treating dreams as a highly important source of information about the unconscious processes—"the dream is the *via regia* [royal road] to the unconscious"—Freud rescued something of the utmost value from the past, where it had seemed irretrievably sunk in oblivion. Indeed, in ancient medicine as well as in the

---

[67] "In Memory of Sigmund Freud," *The Spirit in Man, Art, and Literature,* CW 15, pars. 60f. Freud died in London on September 23, 1939; this essay appeared in a German journal on Oct. 1, 1939.

old religions, dreams had a lofty significance and the dignity of an oracle. At the turn of the century, however, it was an act of the greatest scientific courage to make anything as unpopular as dreams an object of serious discussion. . . . This line of investigation opened the way to an understanding of schizophrenic hallucinations and delusions from the inside, whereas hitherto psychiatrists had been able to describe them only from the outside. [It] provided a key to the many locked doors in the psychology of neurotics as well as of normal people.[68]

Jung's discipleship lasted for almost a dozen years; until, that is, he found Freud's views too restrictive and constrained by dogmatic adherence to the literal sexual significance of virtually everything, from jokes to slips of the tongue, religious rites and mental lacunae. Also, Jung could not accept Freud's almost total disdain for the symbolic.

Much has been written about the relationship between these two giants of modern psychology. And after the published *Freud/Jung Letters,* any interested person can explore it directly. But my intent here is to focus on Jung's thoughts and feelings a mere week after Freud's demise.

After reviewing Freud's debt to his nineteenth-century contemporaries—Charcot, Pierre Janet and Joseph Breuer, internists who worked primarily with the certifiably insane—Jung acknowledges Freud's seminal discoveries in connecting adult neuroses, particularly cases of hysteria, to traumatic infantile fantasies and unconscious *idées fixes* (fixed ideas), which could be effectively treated by "abreaction" (bringing to consciousness repressed emotional re-

---

[68] Ibid., par. 65.

actions through the retelling and reliving of them). But he thought Freud went too far in ascribing all adult fantasy activity to aberrant or buried infantile sexuality. Thus, with the publication of Jung's landmark study, *The Psychology of the Unconscious* (1912),[69] their association came to an abrupt and shadowy end, quite as hurtful, apologetic and mutually regretted as any split between lovers. Forgive me, but it brings to mind this poignant lament familiar to anyone who has ever faced losing a treasured relationship:

> [Streisand and Vince Gill:]
> If you ever leave me, will you take me with you?
> If you're ever lonely, I wanna be lonely too.
> My home's beside you, no matter where you may go.
> My love's inside you, even more than you know.
>
> [Barbra:]
> In a world of anger and lies
> I find peace in your eyes
> A flame in the darkness.
>
> [Both:]
> Ooh, and through all space and time
> 'Till every star refuses to shine
>
> [Barbra:]
> You know where my heart is.
> I'd rather go through any pain love puts us through
>
> [Both:]
> Than to spend one day without you by my side
> If you ever leave me, will you take me with you?

---

[69] Later extensively revised (1950) and republished as *Symbols of Transformation,* CW 5.

If you're ever lonely, I wanna be lonely too, whoa.
My home's beside you, no matter where you may go.

[Barbra:]
Where you may go
[Both:]
My love's inside you, even more than you know.
And I can't remember life without you
The way it used to be
Feels like a million years away.

[Vince:]
Well hold me 'til the angels sing.

[Barbra:]
Tell me every little thing.

[Both:]
Promise me forever from this day
If you ever leave me, will you take me with you?
If you're ever lonely, I wanna be lonely too, whoa.
My home's beside you, no matter where you may go.
Even more than you know.
Even more than you know.[70]

Call me maudlin; I am that too.

Okay, back to business. Jung expresses guarded appreciation for Freud's earlier work, but his derision for the latter's blindness in the area of religious thought and symbolism finally breaks out with some acerbity:

The final application of this theory [i.e., the dogma of infantile sexuality] was to the field of religion, in *The Future*

---

[70] "If You Ever Leave Me," Barbara Streisand and Vince Gill, from *Barbra Streisand: Duets;* written by Richard Marx; ASCAP.

of an Illusion (1927). Though there is much that is still tenable in *Totem and Taboo,* the same cannot, unfortunately, be said of the latter work. Freud's inadequate training in philosophy and in the history of religion makes itself painfully conspicuous, quite apart from the fact that he had no understanding of what religion was about. In his old age he wrote a book on Moses *[Moses and Monotheism]* who led the children of Israel to the Promised Land but was not allowed to set foot in it himself. That his choice fell on Moses is probably no accident in the case of a personality like Freud.[71]

Here, then, is the essence of Jung's criticism:

Freud's psychology moves within the narrow confines of nineteenth-century scientific materialism. Its philosophical premises were never examined, thanks obviously to the Master's insufficient philosophical equipment. So it was inevitable that it should come under the influence of local and temporal prejudices—a fact that has been noted by various other critics. Freud's psychological method is and always was a cauterizing agent for diseased and degenerate material, such as is found chiefly in neurotic patients. It is an instrument to be used by a doctor, and it is dangerous and destructive, or at best ineffective, when applied to the natural expressions of life and its needs.[72]

Holy petunia, you can almost hear the tears fall:

Freud has to be seen against [his] cultural background. He put his finger on more than one ulcerous spot. All that glit-

---

[71] "In Memory of Sigmund Freud," *The Spirit in Man, Art, and Literature,* CW 15, par. 67.

[72] Ibid., par. 70.

tered in the nineteenth century was very far from being gold, religion included. Freud was a great destroyer, but the turn of the century offered so many opportunities for debunking that even Nietzsche was not enough. Freud completed the task, very thoroughly indeed. He aroused a wholesome mistrust in people and thereby sharpened their sense of real values. All that gush about man's innate goodness, which had addled so many brains after the dogma of original sin was no longer understood, was blown to the winds by Freud, and the little that remains will, let us hope, be driven out for good and all by the barbarism of the twentieth century. Freud was no prophet, but he is a prophetic figure. . . . The nineteenth century has left us such a legacy of dubious propositions that doubt is not only possible but altogether justified, indeed meritorious. The gold will not prove its worth save in the fire. Freud has often been compared to a dentist, drilling out the carious tissue in the most painful manner. So far the comparison holds true, but not when it comes to the gold-filling. Freudian psychology does not fill the gap. If our critical reason tells us that in certain respects we are irrational and infantile, or that all religious beliefs are illusions, what are we to do about our irrationality, what are we to put in place of our exploded illusions? Our naïve childishness has in it the seeds of creativity, and illusion is a natural component of life, and neither of them can ever be suppressed or replaced by the rationalities and practicalities of convention.

. . . . In the last resort, each of us carries the torch of knowledge only part of the way, and none is immune against error. Doubt alone is the mother of scientific truth. Whoever fights against dogma in high places falls victim, tragically enough, to the tyranny of a partial truth. All who had a share in the fate of this great man saw this tragedy working out step by step in his life and increasingly narrowing his horizon.[73]

Sigmund Freud, R.I.P., knowing that your heir-apparent loved you like a son, though his fate was to surpass your greatness with humility and a breadth of vision that continues to be mapped.

Enough; I feel a song coming on; something gentle, a trifle melancholy and leading toward a peaceful sleep and helpful dreams. How about this:

> I used to visit all the very gay places
> Those come what may places
> Where one relaxes on the axis of the wheel of life
> To get the feel of life. . .
> From jazz and cocktails.
>
> The girls I knew had sad and sullen gray faces
> With distant gay traces
> That used to be there you could see where they'd been
>   washed away
> By too many through the day. . .
> Twelve o'clock tales.
>
> Then you came along with your siren of song
> To tempt me to madness!
> I thought for a while that your poignant smile was tinged
>   with the sadness
> Of a great love for me.
>
> Ah yes! I was wrong. . .

---

[73] Ibid., pars. 69f.

Again,
I was wrong.

Life is lonely again,
And only last year everything seemed so sure.
Now life is awful again,
A troughful of hearts could only be a bore.
A week in Paris will ease the bite of it,
All I care is to smile in spite of it.

I'll forget you, I will
While yet you are still burning inside my brain.
Romance is mush,
Stifling those who strive.
I'll live a lush life in some small dive...
And there I'll be, while I rot
With the rest of those whose lives are lonely, too. [74]

Jeez. The meaning behind the words, "I love you," is so culturally and personally nuanced these days that you can hardly say it without feeling silly. But I do say it to my paramour, and often; and silly take the hindmost. Here's Natalie again, spelling it out:

L is for the way you look at me,
O is for the only one I see,
V is very very extraordinary,
E is even more than anyone that you adore can love.
It's all that I can give to you
Love is more than just a game for two
Two in love can make it,
Take my heart but please don't break it

---

[74] "Lush Life," from *Natalie Cole: Unforgettable, with Love;* lyrics by Billy Strayhorn; ASCAP.

Love was made for me and you.[75]

I've been asked to say a few words about the difference between projection and true love, or, for that matter, infatuation. It is a thorny issue, but here, for what it's worth, is Edward F. Edinger's response to a similar question, which makes sense to me:

> I think it's distinguished by the degree of consciousness that accompanies it. Love, what I would call object love— as opposed to love based on unconscious factors which always has a degree of possessiveness attached to it—sees the reality of the object and relates to that reality as it is. A person caught up in a transference is not relating to the carrier of that [projection] in his or her full reality at all; he's relating to a piece of his own psychology that he sees in the mirror of the other person. It's a totally different thing.[76]

To that, I can add that I think the proper distinction is rather between being in love and loving. The former involves an obsessive fixation on the partner, usually fueled by lust. When physical passion subsides and projections come home to roost, there remains the possibility of loving the other for who he or she really is, and not who we'd like them to be; and then begins the real challenge of relationship, which is truly measured not by length of service (e.g., 25th, 50th or 60th anniversaries) but by depth of feeling— what the other is worth to you. Like a snowflake or a rainbow, love is evanescent and generally transcends under-

---

[75] "L.O.V.E.," ibid.; words and music by Bert Kaempfert and Milt Gabler; EMI Music,; ASCAP.

[76] "A Conversation with Edward F. Edinger," in *An American Jungian*, p. 44.

standing. But I do believe that long-term relationships depend on a mutual respect and understanding of one's own and the other's typology, complexes and projection.

Of course, that isn't necessarily true; it is just an educated opinion backed by experience. I am no guru with special knowledge. I am the simplest kind of *artifex,* not engaged in alchemical experiments, except metaphorically, and more interested in a nubile *soror mystica* than amassing pots of gold.

I want to give the last words here to Marie-Louise von Franz, Jung's lifelong friend and pupil, who has rather more to say explicitly on the subject than Jung himself. Love, she believes, is about transcending one's littleness:

> Love is such a fateful factor in the life of every human being because, more than anything else, it has the power to release the living from their ego-bound consciousness; it brings us a hint of a transcendental happening, making it possible for us to attend a divine play of the union of Shiva and Shakti, god and goddess, beyond the banality of this earthly life. It is a mystery which no human being has so far penetrated but which is at the same time the goal of life, born anew in each of us. All that we can say is that it is part of a process of reciprocal individuation, of becoming conscious and whole in the encounter. . . .
>
> If we compare the projections that issue from the shadow complex with those proceeding from the anima-animus complex, we may say that insight into one's own shadow projections means first of all moral humiliation, intensive suffering. Insights into projections originating in the anima or the animus, on the other hand, demands not so much humility as level-headedness and common-sense self-

observation and reflection, which demand a certain wisdom and humaneness, because these figures always want to seduce us away from reality into rapture or pull us down into an inner world of fantasy. Whoever cannot surrender to this experience has never lived; whoever founders in it has understood nothing.[77]

---

[77] *Projection and Re-Collection in Jungian Psychology: Reflections of the Soul,* pp. 140ff.

16
Principles of
Practical Psychotherapy

(from *The Practice of Psychotherapy*, CW 16, vintage 1935)

Psychotherapy is not the simple, straightforward method people at first believed it to be, but, as has gradually become clear, a kind of dialectical process, a dialogue or discussion between two persons. Dialectic was originally the art of conversation among the ancient philosophers, but very early became the term for the process of creating new syntheses. A person is a psychic system which, when it affects another person, enters into reciprocal reaction with another psychic system. This, perhaps the most modern formulation of the psychotherapeutic relation between physician and patient is clearly very far removed from the original view that psychotherapy was a method which anybody could apply in stereotyped fashion in order to reach the desired result. It was not the needs of speculation which prompted this unsuspected and, I might well say, unwelcome widening of the horizon, but the hard facts of reality. In the first place, it was probably the fact that one had to admit the possibility of different interpretations of the observed material. Hence there grew up various schools with diametrically opposed views. . . . Each of them rests on special psychological assumptions and produces special psychological results; comparison between them is difficult and often well-nigh impossible.[78]

---

[78] "Principles of Practical Psychotherapy," *The Practice of Psychotherapy,* CW 16, par. 1.

Indeed, the view in the early twentieth century that psycho-therapy was an arcane and useless "method" has long since given way to its acceptance as an effective discipline in dealing with not only neurotic disturbances but also the overall psychic health of anyone eager for self-understanding.

There are of course, as Jung emphasizes, many different schools of thought when it comes to the therapeutic application of psychological verities, from superficial balm to depth analysis. The helping professions, widely unregulated at present, are a dog's breakfast, for sure, and never was the expression *caveat emptor* (buyer beware) more apt. As you would not entrust your ailing pet to a shoemaker, do not put your suffering soul in the hands of a street magician. I mean no disrespect to shoemakers or magicians; just counseling common sense. Choosing a therapist is an intensely personal exercise. It is often said that buying a house and a car are our most significant purchases, but in terms of relationship a therapeutic alliance can be at least as important as a marriage.

> Because neurosis is a developmental disturbance of the personality, we physicians of the soul are compelled by professional necessity to concern ourselves with the problem of personality and the inner voice, however remote it may seem to be. In practical psychotherapy these psychic facts, which are usually so vague and have so often degenerated into empty phrases, emerge from obscurity and take visible shape. Nevertheless, it is extremely rare for this to happen spontaneously as it did with the Old Testament prophets;

generally the psychic conditions that have caused the disturbance have to be made conscious with considerable effort. But the contents that then come to light are wholly in accord with the inner voice and point to a predestined vocation, which, if accepted and assimilated by the conscious mind, conduces to the development of personality.[79]

I believe, as Jung did, that the inner voice is the voice of a fuller life, a wider, more comprehensive consciousness. Yet many people fear the inner voice, and for good reason. It may take them away from loved ones, from safe occupations and a comfortable life. The pursuit of personal integrity requires sacrifices and a tolerance for tension beyond the ordinary. It requires daily attention to behavior, dreams and emotional reactions. Becoming conscious takes time and energy, and a pronounced degree of self-absorption— introspection that is often seen by others as narcissistic and selfish. In an extraverted culture, it is not only "the road less traveled," it is also the path least understood.

So be it. The fuller life, the examined life, is seldom the easier life. More often it brings with it previously unimaginable difficulties, responsibilities and conflicts. But it is for that very reason to be embraced, not eschewed, for a half-life is often worse than no life at all and may drive people to harm themselves or others. Read all about it in the daily newspaper, which is not news to any health professional. The pace of modern life, the busyness, is by its very nature disheartening and can drive one crazy. The stress of surviving in the collective takes a heavy toll on

---

[79] Ibid., par. 316.

individual talents and potential.

What to do about it? Ah, I don't know, for I can get caught up in it as much as anyone. But I cannot resist quoting the following passage from René Daumal's *Mount Analogue,* in which the journey of individuation is pictured as analogous to the perils of mountain climbing:

> Never halt on a shifting slope. Even if you think you have a firm foothold, as you take time to catch your breath and have a look at the sky, the ground will settle little by little under your weight, the gravel will begin to slip imperceptibly, and suddenly it will drop away under you and launch you like a ship. The mountain [the unconscious] is always watching for a chance to give you a spill.[80]

Jung more or less echoes that:

> In fact, the inner voice is a "Lucifer" in the strictest and most unequivocal sense of the word, and it faces people with ultimate moral decisions without which they can never achieve full consciousness and become personalities. The highest and the lowest, the best and the vilest, the truest and the most deceptive things are often blended together in the inner voice in the most baffling way, thus opening up in us an abyss of confusion, falsehood, and despair.[81]

Okay, so once the existence of the unconscious and an inner voice are acknowledged, what next?

Hold on, I'll get there, but first a nap and a foray into the world of romantic love. I have a friend who has just been

---

[80] Mount Analogue: An Authentic Narrative, p. 105.

[81] "The Development of Personality," *The Development of Personality,* CW 17, par. 319.

smitten, and he is as joyful as a cricket on speed. I think nothing beats falling in love, but writing about it comes close.

Men must realize that some women are delicate flowers, not naturally passionate like roses, begonias and gladioli, but potential bloomers to be treated as hybernating orchids or hibiscus. Men generally welcome, and fantasize about, overt displays of lust (call it the slut in their psychic harem, why not). Without some such signals, they may be shy or withdrawn, even impotent, fearing rejection. Of course, this is something for women to be aware of. Men are not prescient, however much women, and men too, wish they were. And both must learn to differentiate candid expressions of desire from vulgar or vampish aggression. The sensitivity of men on this point cannot be overestimated, for the intimidating archetype of the *vagina dentata* lurks in a man's psyche alongside his appreciation of a woman's lust. In general, a man's desire cannot survive a woman's disinterest. He's gotta be pretty thick skinned and over-the-top besotted to try penetrating a brick wall/thorny hedge. And sleeping beauties, however portrayed in fairy tales, can be quite a handful when woken up.

Oh, and both must also know the difference between ravishing and ravaging. Such nuances are the minefields of intimacy. The other day I heard a therapist on the radio comparing a man's sexual response to a woman's. She said a man is like a gas stove—light it and it's ready to go. A woman is more like an electric stove—turn the switch and wait until it warms up. Well, it's an interesting metaphor, but I wouldn't push it as far as my flower analogy.

A delicate flower needs lavish attention to its roots and tender consideration of its fragile petals stretching to the light—the embrace of a longed-for other. Think of it as "romancing the plant." A dear plant needs watering and sun; a dear woman likes to know that she is loved and never tires of hearing it. The response of both requires patience. In daily life as we know it, the transition from the collective street to a safe intimate encounter takes time. Plants wilt, and relationships wither, by inattention to agronomy. Barbra sings her dismay when this happens:

> Here we are,
> Just going through the motions one more time,
> You're lookin' in my eyes, but you don't see me. . .
> Here I am, feeling like a stranger in your arms,
> I touch you, I hold you, but lately I don't know you. . .
> Something is wrong but we go on from day-to-day,
> And we just pretend it all away,
> We act like nothing's changed,
> But in our hearts we know it's not the same. . .
> Cause we're not makin' love anymore,
> Baby we're not makin' love like before,
> We may hold each other tight,
> Say that everything's all right,
> But we're not makin' love. . .
> Remember when you couldn't wait to run into my arms,
> When the love inside my heart was all you needed,
> Remember when you made me wish the night would never
>   end,
> The fire, the thunder, we lived to love each other,
> If ever two hearts were one, then it was yours and mine,
> But that was another place in time,

Now all we have to show,
Are memories of a dream we used to know. . . .
Cause we're not makin' love. . .[82]

So where were we? Oh yes, Jung's lecture/essay on practical psychotherapy. Perhaps I was sidetracked because I've had some dreams lately that I'd rather not go into, here or anywhere else—not even with my analyst. That is a difficult thing to admit, but you see how the shadow works to stay hidden, even in someone who knows better.

But now back to the delicate flower. Think of her as a wannabe bush or tree. Caress her stem, sip her nectars, nibble her petals, stroke every frail tendril. Sing softly to her, as Sinatra does:

I'm gonna love you, like nobody's loved you
Come rain or come shine
High as a mountain, deep as a river
Come rain or come shine
I guess when you met me
It was just one of those things
But don't you ever bet me
cause I'm gonna be true if you let me
You're gonna love me, like nobody's loved me
Come rain or come shine
We'll be happy together, unhappy together
Now won't that be just fine
The days may be cloudy or sunny
We're in or we're out of the money
But I'm with you baby
I'm with you rain or shine.[83]

---

[82] From *Streisand: Greatest Hits;* written by M. Bolton, D. Warren; BMI.

Your aim must be to activate her innate sap, her primitive feminine desire to be transported, cared for and secure from predators (a.k.a., the commotion of her diurnal collective life). This has been a man's role from Day One, his genetic inheritance, and role reversals go against the grain.

This may not be what some feminists like to hear, but that's not my problem.

No, my problem is how to explicate Jung's "Principles of Practical Psychotherapy," which in fact speaks so well for itself that the best I can do is to point that out with some paraphrases and Jung's own words. It is a short lecture but powerful in its simplicity. It is essentially an accolade to the influence of the unconscious in our day-to-day doings and relationships. Jung points out that dream images and synchronistic events hit us over the head, symbolically showing us where we're straying from, or in accord with, our essential path. The trouble is that messages from the unconscious too often fall on deaf ears, since few people know what to listen for, or know the difference between literal and symbolic thinking.[84]

The first principle Jung focuses on is the incapacity to say anything about a man except insofar as he approximates to the "universal man," who is in fact collective man and not an individual personality at all. Thus Jung writes:

> If I wish to treat another individual psychologically at all, I
> must for better or worse give up all pretensions to superior
> knowledge, all authority and desire to influence. I must per-

---

[83] "Come Rain or Come Shine," from *Frank Sinatra: Greatest Love Songs,* written by Harold Arlen and Johnny Mercer; ASCAP.

[84] See *Jung Uncorked,* Book One, chap. 5, pp. 44ff.

force adopt a dialectical procedure consisting in a comparison of our mutual findings. But this becomes possible only if I give the other person a chance to play his hand to the full, unhampered by my assumptions. In this way his system is geared to mine and acts upon it; my reaction is the only thing with which I as an individual can legitimately confront my patient.[85]

This stance produces in the therapist a humility and an attitude that Jung feels is "absolutely necessary because it alone is scientifically responsible," and he goes on—

Any deviation from this attitude amounts to therapy by suggestion, the kind of therapy whose main principle is: "The individual signifies nothing in comparison with the universal." Suggestion therapy includes all methods that arrogate to themselves, and apply, a knowledge or an interpretation of other individualities. Equally it includes all strictly technical methods, because these invariably assume that all individuals are alike.[86]

Jung then observes, with a tone of disappointment, that there are indeed many people who are not only essentially collective but aspire to be nothing but collective:

This accords with all the current trends in education which like to regard individuality and lawlessness as synonymous. On this plane anything individual is rated inferior and is repressed. In the corresponding neuroses individual contents and tendencies appear as psychological poisons. There is also, as we know, an overestimation of individuality based

_____

[85] "Principles of Practical Psychotherapy," *The Practice of Psychotherapy,* CW16, par. 2.
[86] Ibid., par. 3.

on the rule that "the universal signifies nothing in comparison with the individual." Thus, from the psychological (not the clinical) point of view, we can divide the psychoneuroses into two main groups: the one comprising collective people with underdeveloped individuality, the other individualists with atrophied collective adaptation.[87]

The therapeutic attitude therefore must differ accordingly:

A neurotic individualist can only be cured by recognizing the collective man in himself—hence the need for collective adaptation. It is therefore right to bring him down to the level of collective truth. On the other hand, psychotherapists are familiar with the collectively adapted person who has everything and does everything that could reasonably be required as a guarantee of health, but yet is ill. It would be a bad mistake, which is nevertheless very often committed, to normalize such a person and try to bring him down to the collective level. In certain cases all possibility of individual development is thereby destroyed.[88]

The above observations say in effect that everyone is both unique and has a collective side. Go too far in one direction or the other and the psyche rebels by inducing stress to re-balance the personality—just as an introvert's shadow may urge him to mingle with others, or an extravert's other side require a quiet evening reading a book. I am going to an opera tomorrow night precisely in need of that balance.

It is a case of "no one size fits all." Only a careful analysis of conscious and unconscious attitudes can show the proper way out of one-sided neurotic quagmires. Generally

---

[87] Ibid., par. 5.

[88] Ibid.

it is the young who, in demanding to be different, run afoul of the psychological imperative to adapt to their surroundings, while it is the older, socially well-adapted adult who is required to find, or rediscover, his or her creative uniqueness. And it is this latter group who especially benefit from a dialectical procedure in which the analyst does not speak from on high, *ex cathedra,* but acknowledges his bewilderment in the face of the unknown and thereby becomes a fellow participant, not a judge or guru or superior wise person, but as much involved in the process as the so-called patient.

It follows from the above that analysts must make no attempt to bend a patient to their will, or seek to impose a benevolently paternal solution whose consequences they don't have to live with themselves. Permit me to quote Jung at length on this:

> Inasmuch as a man is merely collective, he can be changed by suggestion to the point of becoming—or seeming to become—different from what he was before. But inasmuch as he is an individual he can only become what he is and always was. To the extent that "cure" means turning a sick man into a healthy one, cure is change. Wherever this is possible, where it does not demand too great a sacrifice of personality, we should change the sick man therapeutically. But when a patient realizes that cure through change would mean too great a sacrifice, then the doctor can, indeed he should, give up any wish to change or cure. He must either refuse to treat the patient or risk the dialectical procedure. This is of more frequent occurrence than one might think. In my own practice I always have a fair number of highly cultivated and intelligent people of marked individuality

who, on ethical grounds, would vehemently resist any serious attempt to change them. In all such cases the doctor must leave the individual way to healing open, and then the cure will bring about no alteration of personality but will be the process we call "individuation," in which the patient becomes what he really is. . . . More than one patient has admitted to me that he has learned to accept his neurotic symptoms with gratitude, because, like a barometer, they invariably told him when and where he was straying from his individual path, and also whether he had let important things remain unconscious.[89]

This is Jung's first mention in this essay of the term individuation, but it was clear he was leading up to describing it as an alternative to the traditional therapeutic approach whereby the doctor knows best and tries to "cure," in which process the physician may forget the first tenet of the Hippocratic Oath: Do no harm. Jung explained his attitude to colleagues in England in 1935 as follows:

I naturally try to do my best for my patients, but in psychology it is very important that the doctor should not strive to heal at all costs. One has to be exceedingly careful not to impose one's own will and conviction on the patient. We have to give him a certain amount of freedom. . . . Sometimes it s really a question whether you are allowed to rescue a man from the fate he must undergo for the sake of his further development. You cannot save certain people from committing terrible nonsense because it is in their grain. If I take it away they have no merit. We only gain merit and psychological development by accepting our-

---

[89] Ibid., par. 11.

selves as we are and by being serious enough to live the lives we are trusted with. Our sins and errors and mistakes are necessary to us, otherwise we are deprived of the most precious incentives to development. When a man goes away, having heard something which might have changed his mind, and does not pay attention, I do not call him back. You may accuse me of being unchristian, but I do not care. I am on the side of nature. The old Chinese Book of Wisdom says: "The Master says it once." He does not run after people, it is no good. Those who are meant to hear will understand, and those who are not meant to understand will not hear.[90]

What is the difference between psychotherapy and individuation? Well, simply said, the former involves intervention from outside by a skilled practitioner, while the latter is essentially a process that goes on from the inside out.

Individuation is a simple enough concept to grasp, but the rationale behind it is a mindful stretch. I will let Jung say it:

The phenomenology of individuation is at present almost virgin territory. Hence in what follows I must enter into some detail, for I can only give you an idea of individuation by trying to indicate the workings of the unconscious as revealed in the observed material itself. For, in the process of individual development , it is above all the unconscious that is thrust into the forefront of our interest. The deeper reason for this may lie in the fact that the conscious attitude of the neurotic is unnaturally one-sided and must be balanced by complementary or compensating contents derived from the

---

[90] "The Tavistock Lectures," *The Symbolic Life,* CW 18, par. 291.

unconscious. The unconscious has a special significance in this case as a corrective to the one-sidedness of the conscious mind; hence the need to observe the points of view and impulses produced in dreams, because these must take the place once occupied by collective controls, such as the conventional outlook, habit, prejudices of an intellectual or moral nature. The road the individual follows is defined by his knowledge of the laws that are peculiar to himself; otherwise he will get lost in the arbitrary opinions of the conscious mind and break away from the mother-earth of individual instinct.[91]

In time, *Deo concedente,* the analyst becomes an interested bystander as the role of guide is taken over by compensating contents and attitudes in the unconscious. Now, it must be understood that the unconscious is not an authority to be followed without question. The ego must still mediate the inner voice and take responsibility for actions in the outer world. Remember that when your shadow fancies your neighbor, or you are tempted to downplay your income on a tax return.

I have touched on the process of individuation in Books One and Two of this series, but it behooves me to remind readers of some salient points, namely:

> In general, [individuation] is the process by which individual beings are formed and differentiated; in particular, it is the development of the psychological *individual* as a being distinct from the general, collective psychology.[92]

---

[91] "Principles of Practical Psychotherapy," *The Practice of Psychotherapy,* CW16, par. 12.

[92] "Definitions," *Psychological Types,* CW 6, par. 757.

The aim of individuation is nothing less than to divest the self of the false wrappings of the persona on the one hand, and of the suggestive power of primordial images on the other.[93]

Individuation is a process informed by the archetypal ideal of wholeness, which in turn depends on a vital relationship between ego and unconscious. The aim is not to overcome one's personal psychology, to become perfect, but to become familiar with it. Thus individuation involves an increasing awareness of one's unique psychological reality, including personal strengths and limitations, and at the same time a deeper appreciation of humanity in general. Jung again:

> As the individual is not just a single, separate being, but by his very existence presupposes a collective relationship, it follows that the process of individuation must lead to more intense and broader collective relationships and not to isolation.[94]

> Individuation does not shut one out from the world, but gathers the world to itself.[95]

> Individuation has two principle aspects: in the first place it is an internal and subjective process of integration, and in the second it is an equally indispensable process of objective relationship.[96]

---

[93] "The Function of the Unconscious," *Two Essays,* CW 7, par. 269.

[94] "Definitions," *Psychological Types,* CW 6, par. 758.

[95] "On the Nature of the Psyche," *The Structure and Dynamics of the Psyche,* CW 8, par. 432.

[96] "The Psychology of the Transference," *The Practice of Psychotherapy,* CW 16, par. 448.

Individuation and a life lived by collective values are nevertheless two divergent destinies. In Jung's view they are related to one another by *guilt*. This is a surprising idea, but think about it. Whoever embarks on the personal path becomes to some extent estranged from collective values, but does not thereby lose those aspects of the psyche that are inherently collective. To atone for this "desertion," the individual is obliged to create something of worth for the benefit of society. Jung does not enlarge on what he means by "something of worth," but I believe he would include artistic endeavors of any kind and meaningful work for the common good like locksmithing, plumbing, window cleaning, and perhaps even publishing books. This may sound whimsical, and it is, but listen to Jung:

> Individuation cuts one off from personal conformity and hence from collectivity. That is the guilt which the individuant leaves behind him for the world, that is the guilt he must endeavor to redeem. He must offer a ransom in place of himself, that is, he must bring forth values which are an equivalent substitute for his absence in the collective personal sphere. Without this production of values, final individuation is immoral and—more than that—suicidal. . . .
>
> The individuant has no *a priori* claim to any kind of esteem. He has to be content with whatever esteem flows to him from outside by virtue of the values he creates. Not only has society a right, it also has a duty to condemn the individuant if he fails to create equivalent values, for he is a deserter.[97]

---

[97] "Adaptation, Individuation, Collectivity," *The Symbolic Life,* CW 18, pars. 1095f.

And more pointed:

> Individuation remains a pose so long as no positive values
> are created. Whoever is not creative enough must re-
> establish collective conformity with a group of his own
> choice, otherwise he remains an empty waster and wind-
> bag. Whoever creates *unacknowledged* values belongs to
> the contemned, and he has himself to blame for this, be-
> cause society has a right to expect *realizable* values. For
> the existing society is always of absolute importance as the
> point of transition through which all world development
> passes, and it demands the highest collaborative achieve-
> ment from every individual.[98]

This perspective on guilt as a consequence of individuation is indeed intriguing; and, interestingly enough, Jung
suggests an alternative route to atonement—through love of
soul, inner or outer:

> Outwardly he plunges into solitude, but inwardly into hell,
> distance from God. In consequence, he loads himself with
> guilt. In order to expiate this guilt, he gives his good to the
> soul, the soul brings it before God (the polarized uncon-
> scious) and God returns a gift (productive reaction of the
> unconscious) which the soul offers to man, and which man
> gives to mankind. Or it may go another way: in order to
> expiate the guilt, he gives his supreme good, his love, not to
> the soul but to a human being who stands for his soul, and
> from this human being it goes to God and through this hu-
> man being it comes back to the lover, but only so long as
> this human being stands for his soul. Thus enriched, the
> lover begins to give to his soul the good he has received,

---

[98] Ibid., par. 1098.

and he will receive it again from God, in so far as he is destined to climb so high that he can stand in solitude before God and before mankind.

Thus I, as an individual, can discharge my collective function either by giving my love to the soul and so procuring the ransom I owe to society, or, as a lover, by loving the human being through whom I receive the gift of God.[99]

If I were really audacious, I could suggest this as justification for my vigorous pursuit of Eros after leaving P & G. But I am not so bold as to retrospectively cast my profligacy in such a virtuous light.

Individuation differs from individualism in that the former may deviate from collective norms but retains respect for them, while the latter disdains them entirely. Jung:

A real conflict with the collective norm arises only when an individual way is raised to a norm, which is the actual aim of extreme individualism. Naturally this aim is pathological and inimical to life. It has, accordingly, nothing to do with individuation, which, though it may strike out on an individual bypath, precisely on that account needs the norm for its *orientation* to society and for the vitally necessary relationship of the individual to society. Individuation, therefore, leads to a natural esteem for the collective norm.[100]

The process of individuation, consciously pursued, leads to the realization of the Self as a psychic reality, a center, greater than the ego. Thus individuation is essentially different from the process of simply becoming conscious, a point Jung is at some pains to emphasize:

---

[99] Ibid., pars. 1103f.

[100] "Definitions," *Psychological Types,* CW 6, par. 761.

Again and again I note that the individuation process is confused with the coming of the ego into consciousness and that the ego is in consequence identified with the [S]elf, which naturally produces a hopeless conceptual muddle. Individuation is then nothing but ego-centredness and autoeroticism. But the [S]elf comprises infinitely more than a mere ego, as the symbolism has shown from of old. It is as much one's self, and all other selves, as the ego.[101]

In Jung's view, no one is ever completely individuated. While the goal is wholeness and a healthy working relationship with the Self, one's inner center, the true value of individuation lies in what happens along the way; that is, the pleasure of self-exploration is its own reward:

The goal is important only as an idea; the essential thing is the *opus* [work on oneself] which leads to the goal: *that* is the goal of a lifetime.[102]

It is very late and I'm ever so tired. Let's go to bed with a song in our hearts. How about this:

I stand at your gate.
And the song that I sing is of moonlight.
I stand and I wait
For the touch of your hand in the June night.

The roses are sighing a moonlight serenade.
The stars are aglow.
And tonight how their light sets me dreaming.
My love, do you know

---

[101] "On the Nature of the Psyche," *The Structure and Dynamics of the Psyche,* CW 8, par. 432.

[102] "The Psychology of the Transference," *The Practice of Psychotherapy,* CW 16, par. 400.

That your eyes are like stars brightly beaming?
I bring you, and I sing you a moonlight serenade.

Let us stray 'til break of day
In love's valley of dreams.
Just you and I, a summer sky,
A heavenly breeze, kissin' the trees.

So don't let me wait.
Come to me tenderly in the June night.
I stand at your gate
And I sing you a song in the moonlight.
A love song, my darling, a moonlight serenade.[103]

Jung ends this essay on an optimistic note, thus:

The work done by the patient through the progressive assimilation of unconscious contents leads ultimately to the integration of his personality and hence to the removal of the neurotic dissociation. To describe the detail of this development would far exceed the limits of a lecture.[104]

And I can say no better, except to note that analysis has been called "the impossible profession."[105]

Personally, I wouldn't go that far. Interesting, yes; demanding, too; difficult, often; but certainly possible, and overall gratifying, given humility and the willing participation of analyst and analysand in the Mystery that surrounds anyone's psychological development. Indeed, analysis leads to the realization that one has been unconscious for

---

[103] "Moonlight Serenade," from *Frank Sinatra: Greatest Love Songs;* music by Glenn Miller and Michael Parrish; ASCAP.

[104] "The Principles of Practical Psychotherapy," *The Practice of Psychotherapy,* CW16, par. 27.

[105] See Janet Malcolm, *Psychoanalysis: The Impossible Profession.*

most of one's life. This is a sobering and ego-deflating experience. The upside is finding your personal treasure, the person you were meant to be.

In the end, I think successful psychotherapy comes down to an open mind and the extent to which the therapist has worked on his or her own psychology. In a later essay in this volume of the CW, Jung lays it on the line:

> Each new case that requires thorough treatment is pioneer work, and every trace of routine then proves to be a blind alley. Consequently the higher psychotherapy is a most exacting business and sometimes it sets tasks which challenge not only our understanding or our sympathy, but the whole man. The doctor is inclined to demand this total effort from his patient, yet he must realize that this same demand only works if he is aware that it applies also to himself.[106]

Maktub – it is written.
And so, at last, to bed.

---

[106] "The Psychology of the Transference," *The Practice of Psychotherapy,* CW16, par. 366.

17
The Development
Of Personality

(from *The Development of Personality*, CW 17, vintage 1935)

Jung's basic view of personality is that it refers to aspects of the soul as it functions in the world, aspects that predominantly manifest through the persona. This is a heady mouthful in a deep pool, so I better back up into the shallow end.

For the development of personality, differentiation from collective values, particularly those embodied in and adhered to by the persona, is essential. Jung writes:

> A change from one milieu to another brings about a striking alteration of personality, and on each occasion a clearly defined character emerges that is noticeably different from the previous one. . . . The social character [i.e., persona] is oriented on the one hand by the expectations and demands of society, and on the other by the social aims and aspirations of the individual. The domestic character is, as a rule, moulded by emotional demands and an easy-going acquiescence for the sake of comfort and convenience; when it frequently happens that men who in public life are extremely energetic, spirited, obstinate, wilful and ruthless appear good-natured, mild, compliant, even weak, when at home and in the bosom of the family. Which is the true character, the real personality? . . . .
>
> . . . . In my view the answer to the above question should be that such a man has no real character at all: he is not *individual* but *collective,* the plaything of circumstance and gen-

eral expectations. Were he individual, he would have the same character despite the variation of attitude. He would not be identical with the attitude of the moment, and he neither would nor could prevent his *individuality* from expressing itself just as clearly in one state as in another.[107]

Jung touches briefly on how personality develops from childhood through adolescence to adulthood, but the main thrust of this essay is the abiding question: Who will educate the educators? It is foolish, he believes, to leave the inculcation of personality to those who don't have it.

So, what is personality anyway, and how is it achieved? Jung warns:

The development of personality from the germ-state to full consciousness is at once a charisma and a curse, because its first fruit is the conscious and unavoidable segregation of the single individual from the undifferentiated and unconscious herd. This means isolation, and there is no more comforting word for it. Neither family nor society nor position can save him from this fate, nor yet the most successful adaptation to his environment, however smoothly he fits in. The development of personality is a favour that must be paid for dearly. But the people who talk most loudly about developing their personalities are the very ones who are least mindful of the results, which are such as to frighten away all weaker spirits.

Yet the development of personality means more than just the fear of hatching forth monsters, or of isolation. It also means fidelity to the law of one's own being.[108]

---

[107] "Definitions," *Psychological Types,* CW 6, pars. 798f.
[108] "The Development of Personality," *The Development of Personality,* CW 17, pars. 294f.

Okay, at the risk of repeating myself, let me remind you that personality, in Jung's terms, is the fruit of lengthy introspection and attention to your inner others—especially shadow and animus/anima—and an on-going collaboration with your psychic center, the unseen mover of it all, the Self.

Jung observes that it is "impertinent" to attempt to train a child's personality:

> Personality is a seed that can only develop by slow stages throughout life. There is no personality without definiteness, wholeness, and ripeness. These three qualities cannot and should not be expected of the child, as they would rob it of childhood. It would be nothing but an abortion, a premature pseudo-adult; yet our modern education has already given birth to such monsters, particularly in those cases where parents set themselves the fanatical task of always "doing their best" for the children and "living only for them." This claimant ideal effectively prevents the parents from doing anything about their own development and allows them to thrust their "best" down their children's throats. This so-called "best" turns out to be the very things the parents have most badly neglected in themselves. In this way the children are goaded on to achieve their parents' most dismal failures, and are loaded with ambitions that are never fulfilled. Such methods and ideals only engender educational monstrosities.[109]

Well, that is a pretty strong admonition for any parent to hear, let alone one trying to do his or her "best." Now, I don't think Jung is against lavishing love and attention on our offspring, only warning against foisting on them value systems that may not suit their individual temperament, and so inter-

---

[109] Ibid., par. 288.

fere with their own fledgling process of maturation.

In fact, Jung elucidates the development of personality in much the same terms as earlier outlined in describing the process of individuation:

> No one can train the personality unless he has it himself. And it is not the child, but only the adult, who can achieve personality as the fruit of a full life directed to this end. The achievement of personality means nothing less than the optimum development of the whole individual human being. It is impossible to foresee the endless variety of conditions that have to be fulfilled. A whole lifetime, in all its biological, social, and spiritual aspects, is needed. Personality is the supreme realization of the innate idiosyncrasy of a living being. It is an act of high courage flung in the face of life, the absolute affirmation of all that constitutes the individual, the most successful adaptation to the universal conditions of existence coupled with the greatest possible freedom for self-determination. To educate a man to *this* seems to me no light matter. It is surely the hardest task the modern mind has set itself.[110]

I have hardly begun, and it is suddenly midnight again, the bewitching hour; funny how it creeps up on you, and with MP unavailable, madness beckons. But sit back, I counsel myself; take a deep breath and talk to your inner ensemble to soothe your heartache.

Life is such a whirl! A pox on the Enlightenment and the Industrial Revolution, which are behind all the nonsense about Progress. The pace of modern life is crazy making. But you can choose not to participate—trash your blue- and blackberries, your ipods, iphones and ebooks, your laptops

---

[110] Ibid., par. 289.

and moptops, your HD teevees, your cellphones and emails, your GPS and satellite TV, all that and more. What comes next—an ichip in the forehead or on a fingernail? It makes me shiver just to think about it.

Nobody asks us if we want new or better toys. Call me a Luddite, but I've had the biscuit with modern technology. I am wired up to the gills, inside and out. I have lost track of what is plugged into what and where. If something goes awry, I contact my son's company, sharpconnections.com, which specializes in websites and solving small business computer problems, which I constantly have.

I am tempted to go back to chiseling in stone, only I'm afraid by now I've lost the knack, and my chisel too. I am telling you this to reveal that even analysts can fall into the "poor me" syndrome. We are not superhuman.

I have been morose and thought of escaping it all—and who in this day and age has not wished to be quit of the surrounding cultural madness—but Jeez! I still feel that being alive is an awesome experience. Just walk down the street on a sunny day and you wanna stick around for the lovelies.

For the record, I am as interested in relationship as in making love. But come to that, I think any long-term relationship must have an erotic tinge, however acted out; otherwise, you might as well walk your dog.

Yes, there is more to life than sex—if you have a lover.

> "There's more to life than bread."
> "Not if you're hungry."
> "There's more to life than water."
> "Not if you're thirsty."

- see what I mean?

The world turns, or so we are told, with us on it. Part of the Mystery is that we don't fall off. And the rest—is silence.[111]

The meaning of Hamlet's final soliloquy ending with the now iconic expression, "the rest is silence," is much debated among scholars. But their splitting of hairs does not engage me. I am more concerned with the personality behind such words and what cavernous depths they portend. Here is how the passage goes:

> O, I die, Horatio;
> The potent poison quite o'er-crows my spirit:
> I cannot live to hear the news from England;
> But I do prophesy the election lights
> On Fortinbras: he has my dying voice;
> So tell him, with the occurrents, more and less,
> Which have solicited. The rest is silence.

Shakespeare, you see, has the wit to know that his Hamlet ego is not in charge. He is but a plaything of the gods; his personal drama is but a singular manifestation of a greater back-drop—the archetypal play between love and power, which like as not can happen any time, to anyone. The rest is silence because there is no more to say.

So, make of that what you will, as I now sleep in preparation for another day and coming to grips with another essay.

But did you think I would leave you without a song? Not a chance. Friends encourage me to update my musical lexicon to include rap, hip-hop, reggae, even opera, but that is simply not me. My personality—nurtured by my father's innate love of jazz and popular music, and his life-long affection for my

---

[111] See William Shakespeare, "Hamlet," Act 5, scene 2.

mother, his wife—cleaves to the romantic melodies and lyrics of a bygone age, the mid-twentieth century, like this:

> When somebody loves you, you feel it in your heart
> When somebody loves you, you know it from the start
> Every kiss becomes more than a kiss
> Each look, each touch they mean so much
> And that's when you discover how it feels to be a lover
>
> When somebody loves you, it shows in every smile
> When somebody loves you, your life becomes worthwhile
> Always caring, always sharing everything you do
> When somebody loves you like I love you
> (when somebody loves you, it shows in every smile)
> (when somebody loves you, your life becomes worthwhile)
> Always caring, always sharing everything you do
> When somebody loves you like I love you.[112]

Come to think of it, late as it is, my father's attitude to life had an enormous influence on me, well before and far beyond his regret at my leaving Procter & Gamble. He taught me to accept myself, to appreciate women, to have fun and to stand up for what I believed was right and true. I miss him, realizing anew how lost he was without my mother, whom he outlived by five years. It is beyond me to know if they achieved their potential, but to my mind they both had personality.

> I have been a rover,
> I have walked alone. . . .
> Still and all, I'm happy,
> The reason is, you see,
> Once in a while, along the way,
> love's been good to me.[113]

---

[112] "When Somebody Loves You," from *Frank Sinatra: Romance;* music and lyrics by Sammy Cahn and Jimmy van Heusen; ASCAP.

[113] "Love's Been Good to Me," ibid., music and lyrics by Rod McKuen; ASCAP.

18
Symbols and the
Interpretation of Dreams
(from *The Symbolic Life,* CW 18, vintage 1961)

Sometimes a dream is of such vital importance that its message reaches consciousness no matter how uncomfortable or shocking it may be. From the standpoint of mental equilibrium and physiological health in general, it is much better for the conscious and the unconscious to be connected and to move on parallel lines than for them to be dissociated. In this respect the production of symbols can be considered a most valuable function.[114]

This long essay was originally composed in English and finished shortly before Jung's death in June 1961. It later appeared as the introduction to *Man and His Symbols,* a symposium co-edited by Marie-Louise von Franz and conceived as a popular presentation of Jung's ideas, with contributions by other senior analysts. Jung's essay is comprised of several sections:

1) The Significance of Dreams;
2) The Functions of the Unconscious;
3) The Language of Dreams;
4) The Problem of Types in Dream Interpretation;
5) The Archetype in Dream Symbolism;
6) The Function of Religious Symbols; and
7) Healing the Split.

---

[114] "Symbols and the Interpretation of Dreams," *The Symbolic Life,* CW 18, par. 475.

I will comment briefly on each section, after a few general remarks of my own.

Let me be perfectly frank. Contrary to popular belief, analysts do not interpret dreams. Nor can anyone else. That is a misconception, and it is high time analysts acknowledged this truth and put to shame those advertising their expertise in print and on television. Charlatans can make it sound easy, but you have to be some kind of wizard and highly intuitive to make any sense at all of dreams.

Any analyst worth his or her salt generally finds dreams intriguing but initially impenetrable. The most one can do is circumambulate (walk around) the dream images, garnering associations from the dreamer and amplifying these with historical and mythological parallels—all fodder for a Socratic dialogue. Only the dreamer knows what the dream *means*, and this procedure often brings that to the surface of consciousness. Analysts are not magicians; at best they are guides and facilitators, groping in the same dark as plumbers looking for a leak. My colleagues may flinch at this analogy, but that's the way I see it.

As a matter of fact, an electrician's craft is a more apt analogue, since the analytic focus is on psychic energy (often pictured in dreams as electrical circuitry)—where it's gone, where it wants to go, where it "should" go in order to keep the psychic house healthy. This is the *prima materia,* the base matter, of analytic work, though not with pliers and voltmeters, but with tact, empathy, intuition and Eros. Anything less is regressing to nineteenth-century reductive materialism, as exemplified by traditional Freudian psychoanalysis which, though still prevalent, is nowadays pretty much discredited as a helpful response to psychological distress. *The reductive approach seeks the cause of a symptom; the synthetic or prospective view is more interested in its purpose.*

1. The Significance of Dreams

Jung begins by clarifying the difference between a sign and a symbol.

> Through his language, man tries to designate things in such a way that his words will convey the meaning of what he intends to communicate. But sometimes he uses terms or images that are not strictly descriptive and can be understood only under certain conditions. Take, for instance, the many abbreviations like UN, UNESCO, NATO, etc., which infest our newspapers, or trademarks or the names of patent medicines. Although one cannot see what they mean, they yet have a definite meaning if you know it. Such designations are not *symbols,* they are *signs.* What we call a symbol is a term, a name, or an image which in itself may be familiar to us, but its connotations, use, and application are specific or peculiar and hint at a hidden, vague, or unknown meaning. . . .
>
> A term or image is symbolic when it means more than it denotes or expresses. It has a wider "unconscious" aspect—an aspect that can never be precisely defined or fully explained. This peculiarity is due to the fact that, in exploring the symbol, the mind is finally led towards ideas of a transcendent nature, where our reason must capitulate.[115]

In short, a symbol is the best possible expression for something unknown. Insignia on uniforms, for instance, are not

---

[115] "Symbols and the Interpretation of Dreams," *The Symbolic Life,* CW 18, pars. 416f.

symbols but signs that identify the wearer. Esso, Tide and Pepsodent are signs because they refer to something known. But when gasoline, soap or toothpaste turn up in dreams, they may be symbols, whose meaning can only be determined by the associations of the dreamer together with historical or cultural/mythological amplifications.

Thus, in dealing with unconscious material (dreams, fantasies, etc.), the images can be interpreted either semiotically, as symptomatic signs pointing toward known or knowable facts, or symbolically, as expressing something essentially unknown and yet to be discovered through the dialectical procedure that is the hallmark of depth analysis. As Freud himself reputedly declared, "Sometimes a cigar is just a cigar"—meaning that any pointed object is sometimes just what it is and not necessarily of phallic significance. I think Jung would certainly agree with that.

Now, take the image of a cross, which is ubiquitous in the dreams and drawings of those experiencing a conflict. Then, to a Christian, it may be a sign of Jesus' suffering; but also, on top of, or instead, it can be seen as a symbol of the tension between opposites that the dreamer is experiencing. "My God, my God, why hast thou forsaken me?" is a cry heard not only from religious believers. Conflict is a universal experience, which means it is an archetypal pattern, an inborn template that may manifest in diverse ways on a personal level. The cross is an apt symbol for such an experience.

Jung notes some simple examples of symbolization:

A patient, for instance, confronted with an intolerable situation, develops a spasm whenever he tries to swallow: "He can't swallow it." Under similar conditions another patient

develops asthma: "He can't breathe the atmosphere at home."
A third suffers from a peculiar paralysis of the legs: "He can't
go on any more." A fourth vomits everything he eats: He can't
stomach it." And so on. They could all just as well have had
dreams of a similar kind.[116]

It is in conversation with the analyst that a patient or client
becomes aware of what is behind his or her aberrant behavior
or physical symptom. The non-psychological doctor, of
course, has neither the time nor inclination to listen to a lot of
chatter about what is happening in the patient's life, not to
mention disturbing dreams, and therefore is apt to miss the
unconscious background of the problem.

Freud pioneered the method of free association to dream-
images and fantasies. Jung favored this approach until he realized that you could free-associate to virtually anything and
reach the underlying complex; however, you thereby often
missed the significance of the image itself. He therefore hit on
the principle of circumabulating the image: "What does such-
and-such remind you of?" "And what else?" "And what
else?" In this dogged way the *purpose* of the image might be
discovered.

Jung tells of a man who dreamed that his wife was a vulgar,
drunken shrew, which he insisted in reality she was not.
What, Jung asks, is the unconscious trying to convey by such
an obviously untrue statement?

To understand the import of that dream, Jung called on his
knowledge of a man's inner feminine side, the anima, and his
understanding of the compensatory nature of the unconscious,

---

[116] Ibid., par. 421.

which is central to a belief in the self-regulation of the psyche: when the conscious personality, the ego, is out of whack—as in a conflict situation or a relationship problem—the unconscious may throw up images to correct the imbalance. As it happens, such imagery is often unfathomable, due to the enigmatic, sphinx-like language of the unconscious.

Commenting on the above dream of a man's wife as a shrew, Jung says:

> Subtler minds in the Middle Ages already knew that every man "carries Eve, his wife, hidden in his body." It is this feminine element in every man (based on the minority of female genes in his biological make-up) which I have called the *anima.* "She" consists essentially in a certain inferior kind of relatedness to the surroundings and particularly to women, which is kept carefully concealed from others as well as from oneself. A man's visible personality may seem quite normal, while his anima side is sometimes in a deplorable state. This was the case with our dreamer: his female side was not nice. Applied to his anima, the dream-statement hits the nail on the head when it says: you are behaving like a degenerate female. It hits him hard as indeed it should. One should not, however, understand such a dream as evidence for the *moral nature* of the unconscious. It is merely an attempt to balance the lopsidedness of the conscious mind, which had believed the fiction that one was a perfect gentleman.[117]

Further discourse with the dreamer would then seek to determine where in his daily life his attitude was deficient or required some modification. His wife would not be the central factor in such a discussion, though of course his relationship

---

[117] Ibid., par. 429.

with her would probably come into it.

Although in the early days of medical psychology it was assumed that dreams were analyzed for the purpose of discovering complexes, it is now known that you don't need dream images for that. You get the same result by letting people talk long enough. Well, we all know this from our experience at cocktail parties. Yes, people talk their complexes! Or better said, complexes talk people, revealing emotional disturbances and the tender spots in the psyche, which react to problematic external situations and inner forces beyond our control. With all this in mind, Jung goes on:

> I began to suspect that dreams might have another, more interesting function. The fact that they eventually lead back to the complexes is not the specific merit of dreams. If we want to learn what a dream means and what specific function it fulfils, we must disregard its inevitable outcome, the complex. We must put a check on limitless "free" association, a restriction provided by the dream itself. . . . The dream is its own limitation . . . . There is, for instance, an almost infinite variety of images by which the sexual act can be "symbolized," or rather allegorized. But the dream obviously intends its own specific expression in spite of the fact that the resultant associations will lead to the idea of sexual intercourse. This is no news and is easy to see, but the real task is to understand why the dream has chosen its own individual expression.[118]

Let us now move on to the next section in this essay, where Jung presents substantive evidence for the existence of the unconscious and how it functions.

---

[118] Ibid., par. 433.

2. The Functions of the Unconscious

Jung begins by outlining his "new method" of treating dreams as spontaneous products of the psyche, about which one can assume nothing except that they somehow make sense. Dreams say what they mean and mean what they say; they are not a cloak-and-dagger act covering some secret wish (as Freud believed). They are difficult to understand only because we don't speak their language, not because they are deliberately opaque.

Jung defends the concept of the unconscious thus:

> As to the alleged boldness of the hypothesis that an unconscious psyche exists, I must emphasize that a more modest formulation could hardly be imagined. It is so simple that it amounts to a tautology: a content of consciousness disappears and cannot be reproduced. The best we can say of it is: the thought (or whatever it was) has become unconscious, or is cut off from consciousness, so that it cannot even be remembered. Or else it may happen that we have an inkling or hunch of something which is about to break into consciousness: "something is in the air," "we smell a rat," and so on. To speak under these conditions of latent or unconscious contents is hardly a daring hypothesis.
>
> When something vanishes from consciousness it does not dissolve into thin air or cease to exist, any more than a car disappearing around a corner becomes non-existent. It is simply out of sight, and, as we may meet the car again, so we may come across a thought again which was previously lost.[119]

Then, after debunking the notion that manifestations of the

---

[119] Ibid., pars. 444f.

unconscious are merely symptoms of mental illness rather than "normal occurrences pathologically exaggerated," he goes on to stress the positive value of the unconscious in that its expressions (in dreams, for instance) are not constrained by time or space:

> Just as conscious contents can vanish into the unconscious, other contents can also arise from it. Besides a majority of mere recollections, really new thoughts and creative ideas can appear which have never been conscious before. They grow up from the dark depths like a lotus, and they form an important part of the subliminal psyche. This aspect of the unconscious is of particular relevance in dealing with dreams. One must always bear in mind that dream material does not necessarily consist of memories; it may just as well contain new thoughts that are not yet conscious.[120]

This idea was revolutionary in Jung's time, and is only now being taken seriously by contemporary psychologists of any school who are at a loss to otherwise explain phenomena they are presented with in their consulting rooms.

In broad terms, then, the unconscious consists of both repressed or suppressed contents and subliminal sense perceptions that may surface at any time. Into the latter category falls the phenomenon known as cryptomnesia or "hidden memory"—the recall to consciousness of something whose source has been forgotten and so is thought to be one's own.[121]

---

[120] Ibid., par. 449.

[121] See "Cryptomnesia," *Psychiatric Studies,* CW 1; also *Jung Uncorked,* Book Three, chap. 1, pp. 16ff.

3. The Language of Dreams

This section begins with a comprehensive preamble worth quoting at length:

> All contents of consciousness have been or can become subliminal, thus forming part of the psychic sphere which we call the unconscious. All urges, impulses, intentions, affects, all perceptions and intuitions, all rational and irrational thoughts, conclusions, inductions, deductions, premises, etc., as well as all categories of feeling, have their subliminal equivalents, which may be subject to partial, temporary or chronic unconsciousness. One uses a word or a concept, for instance, that in another connection has an entirely different meaning of which one is momentarily unconscious, and this can lead to a ridiculous or even disastrous misunderstanding. Even a most carefully defined philosophical or mathematical concept, which we are sure does not contain more than we have put into it, is nevertheless more than we assume. It is at the least a psychic event, the nature of which is actually unknowable. The very numbers you use in counting are more than you take them for. They are at the same time mythological entities (for the Pythagoreans they were even divine), but you are certainly unaware of this when you use numbers for a practical purpose.
>
> We are also unconscious of the fact that general terms like "state," "money," "health," "society" etc. usually mean more than they are supposed to signify. They are general only because we assume them to be so, but in practical reality they have all sorts of nuances of meaning. . . . The reason for this variation is that a general notion is received into an individual context and is therefore understood and used in an individual way. As long as concepts are identical with mere words, the variation is almost imperceptible and of no practical impor-

tance. But when an exact definition or a careful explanation is needed, one can occasionally discover the most amazing variations, not only in the purely intellectual understanding of the term, but particularly in its emotional tone and its application. As a rule these variations are subliminal [unconscious] and never realized.

One may dismiss such differences as redundant or over-nice distinctions, but the fact that they exist shows that even the most banal concepts of consciousness have a penumbra of uncertainty around hem, which justifies us in thinking that each of them carries a definite subliminal charge. Although this aspect plays little role in everyday life, one must bear it in mind when analyzing dreams.[122]

Acknowledging and exploring the reality of the unconscious was the touchstone of Jung's life work. The unconscious was as real to him as everyday life. Marie-Louise von Franz recalls that on first meeting Jung (she was eighteen, he was fifty-eight) he referred to a woman he had treated who "lived on the moon." Von Franz asked, "You mean it was as if she lived on the moon?" "No!" declared Jung, "not 'as if,' she *did* live on the moon."[123]

Von Franz was baffled by this statement until she accepted that there is a realm of existence beyond our usual conscious ken. You don't have to be crazy to believe in it, though it helps if you are intuitive and not a hide-bound sensation-type like myself, who tends to believe only in what he can see, hear, smell or touch, a limitation I often feel keenly. I mean, it

---

[122] "Symbols and the Interpretation of Dreams," *The Symbolic Life,* CW 18, pars. 461ff.

[123] James A, Hall and Daryl Sharp., eds. *Marie-Louise von Franz,* pp. 36ff.

was even a leap of faith for me to believe in the unconscious until I had experienced its volcanic eruptions myself.[124]

Jung goes on then to refer to the shock and fright that even highly intelligent people may experience when they have peculiar dreams, involuntary fantasies or visions:

> They assumed that nobody in a sound mental condition could suffer from such phenomena, and that a person who had a vision was certainly pathological. A theologian I knew once avowed his belief that Ezekiel's visions were morbid symptoms, and that when Moses and other prophets heard "voices" they were suffering from hallucinations. Naturally he got into a panic when some spontaneous events of this kind happened to him. We are so used to the rational surface of our world that we cannot imagine anything untoward happening within the confines of common sense. If our mind once in a while does something thoroughly unexpected, we are terrified and immediately think of a pathological disturbance, whereas primitive man would think of fetishes, spirits, or gods, but would never doubt his sanity.[125]

Jung then takes a little poke at Freud:

> Many dreams present images and associations that are analogous to primitive ideas, myths, and rites. These dream-images were called "archaic remnants" by Freud. The term suggests that they are psychic elements left over from times long ago and still adhering to our modern mind. This point of view forms part of the prevailing depreciation of the unconscious as

---

[124] See my books *The Survival Papers: Anatomy of a Midlife Crisis* and *Dear Gladys: The Survival Papers, Book Two.*

[125] "Symbols and the Interpretation of Dreams," *The Symbolic Life,* CW 18, par. 466.

a mere appendix of consciousness or, to put it more drastically, a dustbin which collects all the refuse of the conscious mind—all things discarded, disused, worthless, forgotten, and repressed.

This opinion had to be abandoned in more recent times, since further investigation has shown that such images and associations belong to the regular structure of the unconscious and can be observed more or less everywhere, in the dreams of highly educated as well as illiterate people, of the intelligent as well as the stupid. They are in no sense dead or meaningless "remnants"; on the contrary, they still continue to function and are therefore of vital value just because of their "historical" nature. They are a sort of language that acts as a bridge between the way in which we consciously express our thoughts and a more primitive, more colourful and pictorial form of expression—a language that appeals directly to feeling and emotion.[126]

Jung ends this section with a personal anecdote concerning a "jam" he got into by telling Freud of a dream he had. Freud kept probing for the underlying "wish" behind the manifest dream images. Jung lied to placate Freud, but realized that the debacle happened, as it often does, because of "the personal differences between the analyst and the analysand." He concludes by stressing the importance of the companionable aspect of the analytic encounter:

Dream analysis on this level is less a technique than a dialectical process between two personalities. If it is handled as a technique, the peculiarity of the subject as an individual is excluded and the therapeutic problem is reduced to the simple

---

[126] Ibid., pars. 468f.

question: who will dominate whom? I had given up hypnotic treatment for this very reason, because I did not want to impose my will on others. I wanted the healing processes to grow out of the patient's own personality, and not out of suggestions of mine that would have only a passing effect. I wanted to protect and preserve my patient's dignity and freedom so that he could live his life by his own volition.[127]

4. The Problem of Types in Dream Interpretation

This is an interesting section, but it contains little more than I have uncorked at length elsewhere,[128] so I will move on to uncharted waters.

5. The Archetype in Dream Symbolism

The archetypes of the collective unconscious are at the heart of Jung's approach to an understanding of the psyche. If you don't believe in them and dismiss the unconscious as a chimera, than you are forever locked into living out of the superficial layer of ego-consciousness. This is not necessarily a disaster, but it does hamper individuation and inhibit the development of the personality, as outlined here in the previous chapter. Go ahead, do what you want; I am not a savior, only an interested bystander who once in a while can help people out of holes if they get themselves together enough to help themselves.

This essay assumes no or minimal knowledge of Jung's other writings on the subject. This is no surprise; again and again Jung was obliged to deliver his message in diverse con-

---

[127] Ibid., par. 492.
[128] See *Jung Uncorked,* Book One, chap. 7; ibid., Book Three, chap. 6.

texts to those who were only dimly aware, if at all, of his pro-
digious scientific toils in the clinical field. Thus, repeating
himself was endemic. This caused him in the end to bemoan
his loneliness. Although he had garnered considerable collective acclaim and a global list of appreciative friends, he did
not feel wholly *understood.*[129] He always felt he was about a
hundred years ahead of his time, but I am confident that his
message will continue to gain currency.

Think about it: What other school of psychology appreci-
ates the lodestone of creative resources in the unconscious?
The oceans, or outer space, may rightly be called "the last
frontier"—in the physical world. The psyche, comprising both
consciousness and the unconscious—is another vast world
still in the early stages of exploration by those with the tools,
the interest and the expertise.

Jung begins his discussion of the archetype in dream symbolism:

> The hypothesis we have advanced, that dreams serve the pur-
> pose of *compensation,* is a very broad and comprehensive as-
> sumption. It means that we believe the dream to be a normal
> psychic phenomenon that transmits unconscious reactions or
> spontaneous impulses to the conscious mind. Since only a
> small minority of dreams are manifestly compensatory, we
> must pay particular attention to the language of dreams that
> we consider to be symbolic. The study of this language is al-
> most a science in itself. It has, as we have seen, an infinite va-
> riety of individual expressions. They can be read with the help
> of the dreamer, who himself provides the associative material,
> or context of the dream-image, so that we can look at all its

---

[129] See "Retrospect" in *Memories, Dreams, Reflections,* pp. 355ff.

aspects as if circumambulating it. This method proves to be sufficient in all ordinary cases, such as when a relative, a friend, or a patient tells you a dream more or less conversationally. But when it is a matter of outstanding dreams, of obsessive or recurrent dreams, or dreams that are highly emotional, the personal associations produced by the dreamer no longer suffice for a satisfactory interpretation. In such cases, we have to take into consideration the fact, already observed and commented on by Freud, that elements often occur in a dream that are not individual and cannot be derived from personal experience . . . .

Just as the human body represents a whole museum of organs, with a long evolutionary history behind them, so we should expect the mind to be organized in a similar way rather than to be a product without history. By "history" I do not mean the fact that the mind builds itself up through conscious tradition (language, etc.), but rather its biological, prehistoric, and unconscious development beginning with archaic man, whose psyche was still similar to that of an animal. This immensely old psyche forms the basis of our mind, just as the structure of our body is erected upon a generally mammalian anatomy.[130]

Dear readers, this is difficult stuff and not something you learn from the *Reader's Digest* or simplistic books proposing a technique readily acquired on "how to interpret dreams." But think flexibly and expand your awareness to what is happening below the threshold of consciousness. Jung goes on:

My views about the "archaic remnants," which I have called "archetypes" or "primordial images," are constantly criticized

---

[130] "Symbols and the Interpretation of Dreams," *The Symbolic Life,* CW 18, pars. 521f.

by people who lack a sufficient knowledge both of the psychology of dreams and of mythology. The term "archetype" is often misunderstood as meaning a certain definite mythological image or motif. But this would be no more than a conscious representation, and it would be absurd to assume that such variable representations could be inherited. The archetype is, on the contrary, an inherited *tendency* of the human mind to form representations of mythological motifs— representations that vary a great deal without losing their basic pattern. . . . This inherited tendency is instinctive, like the specific impulse of nest-building, migration, etc. in birds. One finds these *représentations collectives* practically everywhere, characterized by the same or similar motifs. They cannot be assigned to any particular time or region or race.[131]

Consider the motif of the hostile brothers, exemplified in the Biblical story of Cain and Abel, and the initial antagonism between Gilgamesh and Enkidu.[132] Variations of this motif can be found in many historical events, literature and personal experience within families. It is a pattern, like the *puer aeternus* (eternal boy) motif, which can manifest in myriad ways in individual lives, from the thirty-year-old stuck in adolescent behavior to the much older man who still treats his wife as a surrogate for his mother. Archetypes and archetypal motifs are no longer things that have to be proved; they hit us in the face every day if we are open to seeing.

You love her or him, someone socially below or above you, not of your "clan," already "taken," or otherwise inappropri-

---

[131] Ibid., par. 523.

[132] See Rivkah Schärf Kluger, *The Archetypal Significance of Gilgamesh: A Modern Ancient Hero.*

ate. Talk about Romeo and Juliet, this is a scenario enacted all over the world daily. That is why it is an archetypal motif, which, simply said, points to a human situation that is experienced ever and always, everywhere.

Those who find themselves in such situations often despair, feeling they are alone in the dark. Well, they may be in the dark, but they are certainly not alone.

Okay, enough of that heady talk. Now here's a cabaret ditty penned and sung by dear old friends of mine in California. If you can spot the archetypal motif behind it, you win a copy of their new album.

> I dreamed an angel came and drew a picture of my future on the wall;
> An upside-down triangle with three colors splashed around and that was all.
> How can this be a future? Angel answer me before I wake again.
> But the angel only smiled and left me sleeping in the lonely world of men.
> And every day I think about that upside-down triangle in my dream.
> And the pretty little angel who I knew was not exactly what she seemed
> The colors were a dash of blue, a line of green above a splash of red;
> Blue for mind and red for blood and green for all the loves you left for dead.
> And did I wake that day or did I wake in just another kind of sleep?
> Have I ever been awake to see the company a waking man might keep?

Or am I like the child who holds the rod and sees the mirror
of the bait?

A child is born and hooked by time and trouble without
struggle to his fate.

So come back little angel, draw another of your pictures on
my wall.

Tell me I'm alive and well and not some madman's clever
little doll.

Answer me the riddle, tell my crazy heart the things it
wants to know.

Draw another picture angel, where did all my dreams of
Heaven go?

I dreamed a dream, up in the sky and you were there, and
we could fly.

I dreamed a dream, please make it true; that you love me
and I love you.[133]

It is of course a very interesting dream, and I could venture
an interpretation of its images, but the truth is, there is no
analysis outside of analysis. I mean, understanding dreams is
no parlor game; it is a dialectical procedure that can last for
months, even years, given the patience and fortitude of the
two participants.

My longest-standing analysand is a woman in her seventies
who only recently, after seeing me weekly for twenty-five
years, cut back to once a month. It is a delight to hear her un-
pack her dream images and experience the tenacity with
which she tracks the opposites in her emotional reactions to
her everyday life. I learn a great deal from her about the inter-
action between ego and Self.

---

[133] "I Dreamed a Dream," from Rick Jones and Valerie Neale, *Life Drawing,* ©
Half a Brain Music, 2009; ASCAP. See www.RicknVal.com.

6. The Function of Religious Symbols

Jung first bemoans the separation of modern consciousness from the instincts, which nevertheless assert themselves in indirect ways—physical symptoms, accidents, incidents of various kinds, unaccountable moods, unexpected forgetfulness, blunders in speech, synchronistic events and so on.

> Such manifestations show very clearly the *autonomy* of the archetypes. It is easy to believe that one is master in one's own house, but, as long as we are unable to control our emotions and moods, or to be conscious of the myriad secret ways in which unconscious factors insinuate themselves into our arrangements and decisions, we are certainly not the masters. On the contrary, we have so much reason for uncertainty that it will be better to look twice at what we are doing.[134]

> The East has one big myth—which we call an illusion in the vain hope that our superior judgment will make it disappear. This myth is the time-hallowed archetypal dream of a Golden Age or a paradise on earth, where everything is provided for everybody, and one great, just, and wise Chief rules over a human kindergarten. This powerful archetype in its infantile form has got them all right, but it won't disappear from the world at the mere sight of our superior point of view. We even support it by our own childishnesss, for our Western civilization is in the grip of the same mythology. We cherish the same prejudices, hopes, and expectations.[135]

Overall, the thrust of this section is about the price moderns (post-sixteenth century) have paid in losing faith in one or

---

[134] "Symbols and the Interpretation of Dreams," *The Symbolic Life,* CW 18, par. 560.

[135] Ibid., par. 563.

other of the world religions, whose ritual and symbols were once life-saving but are no longer understood.

> While life runs smoothly, the loss remains as good as unnoticed. But when suffering comes, things change very rapidly. One seeks the way out and begins to reflect about the meaning of life and its bewildering experiences. . . . People feel that it makes, or would make, a great difference if only they had a positive belief in a meaningful way of life or in God or immortality. The spectre of death looming up before them often gives a powerful incentive to such thoughts. From time immemorial, men have had ideas about a Supreme Being (one or several) and about the Land of the Hereafter. Only modern man thinks he can do without them. Because he cannot discover God's throne in heaven with a telescope or radar . . . he assumes that such ideas are not "true." I would rather say that they are not "true" enough. They have accompanied human life since prehistoric times and are still ready to break through into consciousness at the slightest provocation.
>
> . . . Since it is a matter of invisible and unknowable things (God is beyond human understanding, and immortality cannot be proved), why should we bother about evidence or truth? . . . There is, however, a strong empirical reason why we should hold beliefs that we know can never be proved. It is that they are known to be useful. *Man positively needs general ideas and convictions that will give a meaning to his life and enable him to find his place in the universe.* He can stand the most incredible hardships when he is convinced that they make sense; but he is crushed when, on top of all his misfortunes, he has to admit that he is taking part in a "tale told by an idiot."[136]

---

[136] Ibid., pars. 565f., italics added.

It is the purpose and endeavour of religious symbols to give a meaning to the life of man. The Pueblo Indians believe that they are the sons of Father Sun, and this belief gives their life a perspective and a goal beyond their individual and limited existence. It leaves ample room for the unfolding of their personality, and is infinitely more satisfactory than the certainty that one is and will remain the underdog in a department store. If St. Paul had been convinced that he was nothing but a wandering weaver of carpets, he would certainly not have been himself. His real and meaningful life lay in the certainty that he was the messenger of the Lord. You can accuse him of megalomania, but your opinion pales before the testimony of history and the *consensus omnium*. The myth that took possession of him made him something greater than a mere craftsman.[137]

You may well ask yourself what is your personal myth? What gives your own life meaning?

7. Healing the Split

This section fittingly sums up pretty much every concern expressed by Jung in his *Collected Works,* and indeed throughout his lifetime.

What is the split he believes needs to be healed?

First and foremost, it is the gap between ego-consciousness and the unconscious, a lacuna that makes us all more or less neurotic, which is to say one-sided and not "at one" with ourselves. Analysis is a practical way to atonement (at-one-ment).

---

[137] Ibid., par. 567; *consensus omnium* = what has always and everywhere been believed.

Second, it is the denigration by our enlightened rationalism of the potentially vital and creative messages from the unconscious in dreams and synchronistic events.

Third, it is the lack of communication between the ubiquitously dominant persona and the shadowy underside of the personality—a lamentable gulf that wreaks havoc on our personal relationships and inhibits our individuation.

Jung begins by differentiating types of symbols:

When the medical psychologist takes an interest in symbols, he is primarily concerned with "natural" symbols as distinct from "cultural" symbols. The former are derived from the unconscious contents of the psyche, and they therefore represent an enormous number of variations on the basic archetypal motifs. . . .

"Cultural" symbols, on the other hand, are those that have expressed "eternal truths" or are still in use in many religions. They have gone through many transformations and even a process of more or less conscious elaboration, and in this way have become the *représentations collectives* of civilized societies. Nevertheless, they have retained much of their original numinosity, and they function as positive or negative "prejudices" with which the psychologist has to reckon very seriously.

Nobody can dismiss these numinous factors on merely rational grounds. They are important constituents of our mental make-up and vital forces in the building up of human society, and they cannot be eradicated without serious loss. When they are repressed or neglected, their specific energy disappears into the unconscious with unpredictable consequences.[138]

---

[138] Ibid., pars. 578ff.

In short, the split in modern life mirrors the dehumanization of mankind through rational, scientific understanding that over the past five hundred years has lost contact with the numinosity of nature and the instinctive wellspring of life:

> Thunder is no longer the voice of a god, nor is lightning his avenging missile. No river contains a spirit, no tree means a man's life, no snake is the embodiment of wisdom, and no mountain still harbours a great demon. Neither do things speak to him nor can he speak to things, like stones, springs, plants, and animals. He no longer has a bush-soul identifying him with a wild animal. His immediate communication with nature is gone for ever, and the emotional energy it generated has sunk into the unconscious.
>
> This enormous loss is compensated by the symbols in our dreams. They bring up our original nature, its instincts and its peculiar thinking. Unfortunately, one would say, they also express their contents in the language of nature, which is strange and incomprehensible to us. It sets us the task of translating its images into the rational words and concepts of modern speech, which has liberated itself from its primitive encumbrances—notably from its mystical participation with things.
>
> At least the surface of our world seems to be purified of all superstitious and irrational admixtures. Whether, however, the real inner world of man—and not our wish-fulfilling fiction about it—is also freed from primitivity is another question. Is not the number 13 still taboo for many people? Are there not still many individuals possessed by funny prejudices, projections, and illusions? A realistic picture of the human mind reveals many primitive traits and survivals.[139]

---

[139] Ibid., pars. 585ff.

Jung's basic message, then, is that our innate fear of the unconscious may be mitigated by becoming alert to its contents, especially as they manifest in dreams.

I am inclined now to have the last word by recounting my initial dream, as we say—the first one I took to an analyst.[140] It went like this:

> I am on a street in the center of an unknown, deserted city, surrounded by cavernous buildings. I am bouncing a ball between the buildings, from one side of the street to another. It kept getting away from me. I could not pin it down. I woke up in a cold sweat, terrified, sobbing uncontrollably.

At this distance it seems quite innocuous, but at the time it had such a powerful effect on me that it utterly changed my life. It was my introduction to the reality of the psyche, a kind of initiation. I was thirty-seven-years old and in the midst of a personal conflict which I had a will to solve, but no way. I kept thinking I could deal with it by myself. But my reaction to the dream—the tears that wouldn't stop, the sleepless nights that followed—destroyed that illusion. I realized I had only two options: blow my brains out or go into analysis. I chose the latter and so have contended with the muddle that is me for many more years.

I called on Rachel, my inner woman, for help.

"Do you recall my initial ball dream?" I asked.

"My memory," she sniffed, "is probably better that that of any of the hundred or so elephants on your mantelpiece."

I nodded, just to keep the piece.

---

[140] I have told the following story elsewhere, in the first volume of the **SleepNot Trilogy,** *Not the Big Sleep: Having fun, seriously,* pp. 107ff, but I cannot expect everyone to have read my other books.

"As I recall," she said, "we came to see that dream in terms of the difficulty you were then having in keeping the opposites in balance. We saw the ball as a symbol of self-containment, and the intent of the dream as evidence for the ongoing, self-regulating process in the psyche. The fact that the ball kept getting away from you underlined the fact that you were not in control. Right? And balls, in case you've forgotten, are symbols of the Self."

I nodded. It was all coming back to me.

"Yes, oh yeah," I said. "I was bursting out in all directions, not at all contained. I was the epitome of collective man. My Bible was Dale Carnegies's *How To Win Friends and Influence People*. I was an extraverted, hail-fellow well-met. I did not have a thought I could call my own and no personal center. I had a wife and three children and more girlfriends than Hugh Hefner. I grew my own Fineglow in our suburban vegetable patch, right behind the corn. I got high at a Rolling Stones concert and fell into bed with my secretary. My life was so compartmentalized that I didn't have a clue who was me."

I put my head down and wept.

"Silly Billy!" snapped Rachel. "Wake up! That was years ago. If that dream still affects you, we have work to do. What is currently going on in your life that is in some way similar to what you went through thirty years ago? What change are you resisting?"

Fair questions. I mopped up my tears and wracked my brain. Nothing came to mind. I mean, thirty years ago I was on my knees. Now I wasn't, and hadn't been for as long as I could remember. Sure, from time to time I hobble along with sore legs, a back ache or stiff neck, but who doesn't; stress is the price we pay for being civilized. There are so many palliatives for our physical ailments —and so many views on what causes or cures, that if we took such things to heart we would be walking pharmaceuticals. And diets? Don't get me started. I trust my body and that's my bottom line.

"I leave you to it," said Rachel, and disappeared.

Sometimes she does that. Just when you think she's about to solve all your problems, she goes into hiding. It's really annoying, but she's her own person; that's just the way it is.

Okay, I got down to brass tacks. In order to put into perspective my current situation, I did a mental inventory of my progression through life, dividing the various stages acronymically as follows:

—PP (prepuberty, about which I remember very little);

—AD (adolescence, when my hormones were so active I could hardly eat);

—YA (young adult, when my hormones were so active I would have a go at a chicken);

—PR (parent responsibilities, which I thoroughly enjoyed);

—PM (post-marriage, which I enjoyed even more);

—FMV (finding my vocation, which has sustained me).

Overall, the broader divisions in my life have been BA (before analysis) and AA (after analysis). Of what went on in the BA period I often need to be reminded, which my now grown-up children are not loath to do—though kindly, I should say, without acrimony. The AA period usually takes care of itself, being well represented in terms of my current activities—writing, publishing and practicing as an analyst.

Anyway, the point I meant to make before I got sidetracked is that life is now so complicated, and we're bombarded with so much pain and sorrow in the world that we can do hardly anything about, that it's a wonder we can function at all. Just to read the daily newspaper would reduce a statue to tears.

There, I got off track again. Where was I; oh yes, Rachel's queries: What is going on now in my life that is similar to what brought me to my knees so many years ago? What change might I be resisting? They were lofty questions.

The thing, is, there was so much going on in my head and my house that I had to get away to come to grips with answers. No sooner thought than done: I booked a room in a posh resort lodge on Georgian Bay in northern Ontario and packed a bag. I took my dog-eared traveling set of Jung's Collected Works, which I never go anywhere without, and a few pot-boilers just in case. I took my loaded iPod. I did not take my lap-top Mac and I didn't call in for messages. Every morning I did lengths in the pool and then lay back in the hot tub. I had a daily massage and Alicia gave me my first-ever pedicure. I wallowed in good mother.

I stayed there for seven days and seven nights. I went for long walks and stared at the wall. I had several conversations with Rachel, who was more than helpful. It was off-season, so there weren't many other guests. I dined and chatted with a Japanese couple and an old gent who lost a leg at Dieppe. I did not come across any lovelies (well, other than the fair Alicia, honor bound not to frolic with her clients); lucky me again, because for sure that would have distracted me from what I was there for. Over and over I listened to Frank Sinatra belting out love songs.

Never thought I'd fall,
But now I hear love's call.
I'm getting sentimental over you.
Things you say and do,
Just thrill me through and through,
I'm getting sentimental over you.[141]

And this:

Do you love me, as I love you,
Are you my life to be, my dream come true.
Or will this dream of mine
Fade out of sight
Like the moon growing dim,
On the rim of the hill
In the chill, chill, chill, still of the night.[142]

By the end of the week I knew what I had to do. Like a general marshaling his forces, I laid out a plan of action. I felt good. I slept easy. I could smile again.

Back in the city, I took steps to make actual what for me was truly an unexpected enantiodromia—the emergence of the unconscious opposite in the course of time. Or you can call it the transcendent function; that's true too.

Timing is everything. *Kairos.*

---

[141] "I'm Getting Sentimental Over You," lyrics by George Bassman and New Washisugton; BMI.

[142] "In the Still of the Night," lyrics by Arthur Schwartz and Howard Dietz; BMI.

Marie-Louise von Franz and C. G. Jung (about 1960).

Afterword

This concludes Book Four of *Jung Uncorked,* and it is possibly the end of my explicating essays in Jung's *Collected Works.* There remain many other essays I haven't focused on, but I don't know that I have the energy for another round. On the other hand, uncorking Jung's vintages keeps me close to him and is a good container for my style of self-expression that favors Eros as much as Logos.

Time will tell.

Let the final words here be from Jung's autobiography:

I falter before the task of finding the language which might adequately express the incalculable paradoxes of love. Eros is a *kosmogonos,* a creator and father-mother of all higher consciousness. I sometimes feel that Paul's words—"Though I speak with the tongues of men and of angels, and have not love" [1 Cor. 13:1]—might well be the first condition of all cognition and the quintessence of divinity itself. . . . In my medical experience as well as in my own life I have again and again been faced with the mystery of love, and have never been able to explain what it is. . . . Love "bears all things" and "endures all things" (1 Cor. 13:7). These words say all there is to be said; nothing can be added to them. For we are in the deepest sense the victims and the instruments of cosmogonic "love." Man can try to name love, showering upon it all the names at his command, and still he will involve himself in endless self-deceptions.[143]

---

[143] *Memories, Dreams, Reflections,* pp. 353f.

Or, on a different level, a warning from Jung:

So far as I can see, no relevant objection could be raised from the Christian point of view against anyone accepting the task of individuation imposed on us by nature, and the recognition of our wholeness or completeness, as a binding personal commitment. If he does this consciously and intentionally, he avoids all the unhappy consequences of repressed individuation. In other words, if he voluntarily takes the burden of completeness on himself, he need not find it "happening" to him against his will in a negative form. This is as much as to say that anyone who is destined to descend into a deep pit had better set about it with all the necessary precautions rather than risk falling into the hole backwards.[144]

---

[144] "Christ, A Symbol of the Self," *Aion,* CW 9ii, par. 125.

Bibliography

Adler, Alfred. *The Individual Psychology of Alfred Adler.* Ed. H. Ansbacher and R. Ansbacher. New York: Basic Books, 1956.

Aristophenes. *Lysistrata.* New York: Dover Thrift Ed., 1980.

Bulfinch, Thomas. *Bulfinch's Mythology: The Age of Fable.* Garden City, NY: Doubleday & Company, 1968.

Carotenuto, Aldo. *Eros and Pathos: Shades of Love and Suffering.* Toronto: Inner City Books, 1989.

Colombo, John Robert. *Colombo's All-Time Great Canadian Quotations.* Toronto: Stoddart, 1994.

Daumal, René. *Mount Analogue: An Authentic Narrative.* Trans. Roger Shattuck. London, UK: Vincent Stuart Ltd., 1959.

Dostoyevsky, Fyodor. *Notes from Underground.* Trans. Andrew McAndrew. New York: Signet, 1961.

Dourley, John P. *The Illness That We Are: A Jungian Critique of Christianity.* Toronto: Inner City Books, 1984.

_____. *A Strategy for a Loss of Faith.* Toronto: Inner City Books, 1992.

Edinger, Edward F. *Anatomy of the Psyche: Alchemical Symbolism in Psychotherapy.* La Salle, IL: Open Court, 1985.

_____. *The Creation of Consciousness: Jung's Myth for Modern Man.* Toronto: Inner City Books, 1984.

_____. "M. Esther Harding, 1888-1971." In *Spring 1972.* Zurich: Spring Publications, 1972.

_____. *The Mysterium Lectures: A Journey Through Jung's*

147

Mysterium Coniunctionis. Toronto: Inner City Books, 1995.

_____. *The Mystery of the Coniunctio: Alchemical Image of Individuation.* Toronto: Inner City Books, 1994.

_____. *Science of the Soul: A Jungian Perspective.* Toronto: Inner City Books, 2002.

Ellenberger, Henri. *The Discovery of the Unconscious.* New York: Basic Books, 1970.

Freud, Sigmund. *New Introductory Lectures on Psycho-Analysis* (1933), lecture 21. In *The Complete Psychological Works of Sigmund Freud.* Ed. James Strachey. London, UK: The Hogarth Press, 1978.

_____. *Moses and Monotheism.* New York: Vintage Books (Alfred A. Knopf Inc. and Random House), 1939, 1967.

Frey-Rohn, Liliane. *From Freud to Jung: A Comparative Study of the Psychology of the Unconscious.* Boston: Shambhala Publications, 1974.

Hall, James A., and Sharp, Daryl, eds. *Marie-Louise von Franz: The Classic Jungian and the Classic Jungian Tradition.* Toronto: Inner City Books, 2008.

Hannah, Barbara. *Jung: His Life and Work (A Biographical Memoir).* New York: Capricorn Books, G.P. Putnam's Sons, 1976.

Harding, M. Esther. *The Way of All Women: A Psychological Interpretation.* London, UK: Rider & Company, 1971.

Hollis, James. *The Middle Passage: From Misery to Meaning in Midlife.* Toronto: Inner City Books, 1993.

_____. *The Eden Project: In Search of the Magical Other.* Toronto: Inner City Books, 1998.

_____. *Under Saturn's Shadow: The Wounding and Healing of Men.* Toronto: Inner City Books, 1994.

Jacoby, Mario. *The Analytic Encounter: Transference and Human Relationship.* Toronto: Inner City Books, 1984.

_____. *Longing for Paradise: Psychological Perspectives on an Archetype.* Toronto: Inner City Books, 2006.

Jaffe, Lawrence W. *Liberating the Heart: Spirituality and Jungian Psychology.* Toronto: Inner City Books, 1990.

Jones, Rick, and Neale, Valerie. *Life Drawing.* CD; ASCAP; © Half a Brain Music, 2009; www.RicknVal.com.

Jung, C. G. *C. G. Jung Letters.* (Bollingen Series XCV). 2 vols. Ed. G. Adler and A. Jaffé. Princeton: Princeton University Press, 1973.

_____. *The Collected Works of C. G. Jung* (Bollingen Series XX). 20 vols. Trans. R. F. C. Hull. Ed. H. Read, M. Fordham, G. Adler, Wm. McGuire. Princeton: Princeton University Press, 1953-1979.

_____. *Memories, Dreams, Reflections.* Ed. Aniela Jaffé. New York: Pantheon Books, 1961.

_____. *Visions: Notes of the Seminar Given in 1930-1934* (Bollingen Series XCIX). 2 vols. Ed. Claire Douglas. Princeton: Princeton University Press, 1997.

Jung, Carl G., and von Franz, Marie-Louise, eds. *Man and His Symbols.* London, UK: Aldus Books, 1964.

Kluger, Rivkah Schärf. *The Archetypal Significance of Gilgamesh:*

A Modern Ancient Hero. Ed. H. Yehezkel Kluger. Einsiedeln, Switzerland: Daimon Verlag, 1991.

Kreinheder, Albert. *Body and Soul: The Other Side of Illness.* 2nd edition. Toronto: Inner City Books, 2008.

Malcolm, Janet. *Psychoanalysis: The Impossible Profession.* New York: Alfred A. Knopf, 1981.

McGuire, William, ed. *The Freud/Jung Letters* (Bollingen Series XCIV). Trans. Ralph Manheim and R.F.C. Hull. Princeton: Princeton University Press, 1974.

McGuire, William, and Hull, R.F.C., eds. *C. G. Jung Speaking: Interviews and Encounters* (Bollingen Series XCVII. Princeton: Princeton University Press, 1977.

Meredith, Margaret Eileen. *The Secret Garden: Temenos for Individuation.* Toronto: Inner City Books, 2005.

Monick, Eugene. *Phallos: Sacred Image of the Masculine.* Toronto: Inner City Books, 1987.

Onians, R.B. *The Origins of European Thought.* Cambridge, MA: Cambridge University Press, 1951.

Perera, Sylvia Brinton. *Descent to the Goddess: A Way of Initiation for Women.* Toronto: Inner City Books, 1981.

Qualls-Corbett, Nancy. *The Sacred Prostitute: Eternal Aspect of the Feminine.* Toronto: Inner City Books, 1988.

Rank, Otto. *The Trauma of Birth.* New York: Brunner, 1952.

Rilke, Rainer Maria. *The Notebook of Malte Laurids Brigge.* Trans. John Linton. London, UK: The Hogarth Press, 1959.

_____. *Rilke on Love and Other Difficulties.* Ed. John Mood.

New York, Norton, 1975.

Sharp, Daryl. *Chicken Little: The Inside Story (a Jungian romance).* Toronto: Inner City Books, 1993.

_____. *Dear Gladys: The Survival Papers, Book. 2.* Toronto: Inner City Books, 1989.

_____. *Eyes Wide Open: Late Thoughts (a Jungian romance).* Toronto: Inner City Books, 2007.

_____. *Getting To Know You: The Inside Out of Relationship.* Toronto: Inner City Books, 1992.

_____. *Jung Lexicon: A Primer of Terms and Concepts.* Toronto: Inner City Books, 1991.

_____. *Jung Uncorked: Rare Vintages from the Cellar of Analytical Psychology.* 4 vols. Toronto: Inner City Books, 2008-9.

_____. *Jungian Psychology Unplugged: My Life as an Elephant.* Toronto, Inner City Books, 1998.

_____. *Living Jung: The Good and the Better.* Toronto: Inner City Books, 1996.

_____. *Not the Big Sleep: On Having Fun, Seriously (a Jungian romance).* Toronto: Inner City Books, 2005.

_____. *On Staying Awake: Getting Older and Bolder (another Jungian romance).* Toronto: Inner City Books, 2006.

_____. *Personality Types: Jung's Model of Typology.* Toronto: Inner City Books, 1987.

_____. *The Secret Raven: Conflict and Transformation in the Life of Franz Kafka.* Toronto: Inner City Books, 1980.

_____. *The Survival Papers: Anatomy of a Midlife Crisis.* Toronto: Inner City Books, 1988.

_____. *Who Am I, Really? Personality, Soul and Individuation.* Toronto: Inner City Books, 1995.

Sparks, J. Gary. *At the Heart of Matter: Synchronicity and Jung's Spiritual Testament.* Toronto: Inner City Books, 2007.

Stevens, Anthony. *Archetype Revisited: An Updated Natural History of the Self.* Toronto: Inner City Books, 2003.

Storr, Anthony. *Solitude.* London, UK: HarperCollins Publishers, 1997.

Thurber, James, *The Thurber Carnival.* New York: Harper and Brothers, 1931.

Vanier, Jean. *Befriending the Stranger.* Toronto: Novalis, 2005.

von Franz, Marie-Louise. *Alchemy: An Introduction to the Symbolism and the Psychology.* Toronto: Inner City Books, 1980.

_____. *Animus and Anima in Fairy Tales.* Toronto: Inner City Books, 2002.

_____. *C. G. Jung: His Myth in Our Time.* Toronto: Inner City Books, 1998.

_____. *On Divination and Synchronicity.* Toronto: Inner City Books, 1980.

_____. *The Problem of the Puer Aeternus.* Revised ed. Ed. Daryl Sharp. Toronto: Inner City Books, 2000.

_____. *Projection and Re-Collection in Jungian Psychology: Reflections of the Soul.* Trans. William H. Kennedy. La Salle, IL: Open Court, 1980.

_____. *A Psychological Interpretation of the Golden Ass of Apuleius: The Liberation of the Feminine in Man.* Revised ed. Boston: Shambhala Publications, 1992.

_____. *Redemption Motifs in Fairy Tales.* Toronto: Inner City Books, 1980.

Von Franz, Marie-Louise, ed. with commentary. *Aurora Consurgens: A Document Attributed to Thomas Aquinas on the Problem of Opposites in Alchemy.* Toronto: Inner City Books, 2000.

Von Franz, Marie-Louise, and Hillman, James. *Jung's Typology.* New York: Spring Publications, 1971.

Walker, Alice. *In the Light of My Father's Smile.* New York: Random House, Ballantine Books, 1998.

Wilhelm, Richard, trans. *The I Ching or Book of Changes.* Rendered into English by Cary F. Baynes. London, UK: Routledge & Kegan Paul, 1968.

Wolff, Toni. *Structural Forms of the Feminine Psyche.* Zurich: C. G. Jung Institute, 1985.

Woodman, Marion. *Addiction to Perfection: The Still Unravished Bride.* Toronto: Inner City Books, 1982.

_____. *Conscious Femininity: Interviews with Marion Woodman.* Toronto: Inner City Books, 1993.

_____. *The Owl Was a Baker's Daughter: Obesity, Anorexia Nervosa and the Repressed Feminine.* Toronto: Inner City Books, 1980.

_____. *The Pregnant Virgin: A Process of Psychological Transformation.* Toronto: Inner City Books, 1985.

Index

154

Also in this Series by Daryl Sharp

Please see next page for discounts and postage/handling.

THE SECRET RAVEN
Conflict and Transformation in the Life of Franz Kafka
ISBN 978-0-919123-00-7. (1980) 128 pp. $25

PERSONALITY TYPES: Jung's Model of Typology
ISBN 978-0-919123-30-9. (1987) 128 pp. **Diagrams** $25

THE SURVIVAL PAPERS: Anatomy of a Midlife Crisis
ISBN 978-0-919123-34-2. (1988) 160 pp. $25

DEAR GLADYS: The Survival Papers, Book 2
ISBN 978-0-919123-36-6. (1989) 144 pp. $25

JUNG LEXICON: A Primer of Terms and Concepts
ISBN 978-0-919123-48-9. (1991) 160 pp. **Diagrams** $25

GETTING TO KNOW YOU: The Inside Out of Relationship
ISBN 978-0-919123-56-4. (1992) 128 pp. $25

THE BRILLIG TRILOGY:

1. CHICKEN LITTLE: The Inside Story *(A Jungian romance)*
ISBN 978-0-919123-62-5. (1993) 128 pp. $25

2. WHO AM I, REALLY? Personality, Soul and Individuation
ISBN 978-0-919123-68-7. (1995) 144 pp. $25

3. LIVING JUNG: The Good and the Better
ISBN 978-0-919123-73-1. (1996) 128 pp. $25

JUNGIAN PSYCHOLOGY UNPLUGGED: My Life as an Elephant
ISBN 978-0-919123-81-6. (1998) 160 pp. $25

DIGESTING JUNG: Food for the Journey
ISBN 978-0-919123-96-0. (2001) 128 pp. $25

JUNG UNCORKED: Rare Vintages from the Cellar of Analytical Psychology
Four books. ISBN 978-1-894574-21-1/22-8/24-2 (2008-9) 128 pp. each. $25 each

THE SLEEPNOT TRILOGY:

1. NOT THE BIG SLEEP: On having fun, seriously *(A Jungian romance)*
ISBN 978-0-894574-13-6. (2005) 128 pp. $25

2. ON STAYING AWAKE: Getting Older and Bolder *(Another Jungian romance)*
ISBN 978-0-894574-16-7. (2006) 144 pp. $25

3. EYES WIDE OPEN: Late Thoughts *(Another Jungian romance)*
ISBN 978-0-894574-18-1. (2007) 160 pp. $25

Studies in Jungian Psychology
by Jungian Analysts

Quality Paperbacks

Prices and payment in $US (except in Canada, $Cdn)

Jung and Yoga: The Psyche-Body Connection
Judith Harris (London, Ontario) ISBN 978-0-919123-95-3. 160 pp. $25

The Gambler: Romancing Lady Luck
Billye B. Currie (Jackson, MS) 978-1-894574-19-8. 128 pp. $25

Conscious Femininity: Interviews with Marion Woodman
Introduction by Marion Woodman (Toronto) ISBN 978-0-919123-59-5. 160 pp. $25

The Sacred Psyche: A Psychological Approach to the Psalms
Edward F. Edinger (Los Angeles) ISBN 978-1-894574-09-9. 160 pp. $25

Eros and Pathos: Shades of Love and Suffering
Aldo Carotenuto (Rome) ISBN 978- 0-919123-39-7. 144 pp. $25

Descent to the Goddess: A Way of Initiation for Women
Sylvia Brinton Perera (New York) ISBN 978-0-919123-05-2. 112 pp. $25

Addiction to Perfection: The Still Unravished Bride
Marion Woodman (Toronto) ISBNj 978-0-919123-11-3. Illustrated. 208 pp. $30/$35hc

The Illness That We Are: A Jungian Critique of Christianity
John P. Dourley (Ottawa) ISBN 978-0-919123-16-8. 128 pp. $25

Coming To Age: The Croning Years and Late-Life Transformation
Jane R. Prétat (Providence) ISBN 978-0-919123-63-2. 144 pp. $25

Jungian Dream Interpretation: A Handbook of Theory and Practice
James A. Hall, M.D. (Dallas) ISBN 978-0-919123-12-0. 128 pp. $25

Phallos: Sacred Image of the Masculine
Eugene Monick (Scranton) ISBN 978-0-919123-26-7. 30 illustrations. 144 pp. $25

The Sacred Prostitute: Eternal Aspect of the Feminine
Nancy Qualls-Corbett (Birmingham) ISBN 978-0-919123-31-1. Illus. 176 pp. $30

Longing for Paradise: Psychological Perspectives on an Archetype
Mario Jacoby (Zurich) ISBN 978-1-894574-17-4. 240 pp. $35

The Pregnant Virgin: A Process of Psychological Development

Marion Woodman (Toronto) ISBN 978-0-919123-20-5. Illustrated. 208 pp. $30pb/$35hc

<u>*Discounts:*</u> *any 3-5 books, 10%; 6-9 books, 20%; 10-19, 25%; 20 or more, 40% .*

<u>*Add Postage/Handling:*</u> *1-2 books, $6 surface ($10 air); 3-4 books, $8 surface*

($12 air); 5-9 books, $15 surface ($20 air); 10 or more, $15 surface ($30 air)

<u>Visa credit cards accepted. Toll-free: Tel. 1-888-927-0355; Fax 1-888=924-1814.</u>

INNER CITY BOOKS, Box 1271, Station Q, Toronto, ON M4T 2P4, Canada
Tel. (416) 927-0355 / Fax (416) 924-1814 / booksales@innercitybooks.net